LEGENDS OF FLIGHT:

LOWRY HERITAGE

BY

JOHN BOND AND GEORGE PAXTON

WINGS OVER THE ROCKIES AIR AND SPACE MUSEUM
DENVER, COLORADO

Published – 2017 by Wings over the Rockies Air and Space Museum, John Bond, George Paxton

Printed by Morrell Printing

Lafayette, Colorado

ISBN 978-1-5323-3052-0

For
The volunteers at Wings
A great group
Who serve with unlimited devotion

Contents

Preface

What is this Book? It is a collection of facts and figures of people and events intended to inform, educate and perhaps inspire. It is centered around aviation history and Lowry heritage, but certainly not limited to it.

The book began with a steno pad and a passion for history. During John Bond's service in the Army/Air Force, he had three postings to Lowry. When he retired, he and Grace bought a house literally across the street from the base. He became involved in the Lowry Heritage Museum and then Wings over the Rockies, serving on the board and as historian. Lowry is part of his psyche and he in turn is part of Lowry's. Whenever John came across a fact about the base, about flying, about historical dates or events that he felt were important, he would make a hand written entry in a 6 by 8 inch steno pad. Eventually, the notations covered a period from 1861 to 2003.

When I became a volunteer at Wings in 2004, I joined John in the Photo Archives Section. The steno pad was used at that time as a reference document, John to reaffirm some fact from the past and I to learn as much about Lowry and the museum as I could, as fast as I could.

As time passed we both realized that this steno pad was a valuable document in bringing the past to light. The first step was to have it typed and placed in a larger format, a three ring binder. Areas that were succinct needed to be expanded for readability and thorough understanding. Corrections (very few) needed to be made. Research led us into related areas. New material was added. Slowly but surely it became a book.

In 2013, along with Jack Ballard, John and I produced "Lowry Air Force Base" for Arcadia Publishing's "Images of America" series. The idea of that book was not only to tell the Lowry Story but also to share with the reader some of our immense photo collection for the first time.

The goals of this book are similar; to entertain and to inform. It is a collection of exploration, of research and of personal experience. We have ranged from the most significant (President Truman's armed forces desegregation order in 1948) to the trivial (the shape of the windows on the Columbine II aircraft vs. the Columbine III). It is used in our photo archives section almost daily.

We are certain the book is not without mistakes, now and most assuredly in the future. History is not static. New information is constantly challenging old beliefs. If history were set in stone, publishers of non-fiction books could shut down their presses.

John Bond's and my love is history. We hope this book will inform and hopefully inspire you to join us in the exciting world of Lowry, aviation and beyond.

George Paxton
Denver, Colorado

Chapter 1
Beginning to 1930

1861-1863

Early attempts to use balloons for reconnaissance were made during the civil war. Thaddeus Lowe, (1832-1913) a well known balloonist, was selected as the chief aeronaut for the Union Army Balloon Corps. The Balloon Corps served at Seven Pines, Antietam, Fredericksburg and other lesser battles. Lowe and the others members served by contract and were never part of the army. The Corps was disbanded in 1863 following the resignation (due to a salary dispute) of Lowe. The G.W Parke Curtis, a converted coal barge with gas generators and a balloon, is credited with being the world's first aircraft carrier. A military balloon, the "Santiago" built at Fort Logan by Ivy Baldwin, saw limited action in the Spanish American War. By then the balloons were in the Signal Corps. Over the years the Balloon corps had various names such as Bureau of Photographic Engineers, Quartermaster Corps, Corps of Engineers, and Signal Corps.

1864

Dec.18 – Francis Lowry's father, Walter Bingham Lowry (1864-1953),was born. Walter Lowry was deputy mayor of Denver and manager of improvement and parks under Mayor George D. Begoli in the 30s. Nell French Lowry was born on 6 Sept.,1865. Died 1958.

1885

Baron Von Richthofen joined Mathias P. Cochrane in the Montclair Town and Improvement Co. The Town was incorporated and platted in 1888. Cochrane was the first mayor. He resigned due to ill health and passed away shortly. The Baron (Manfred Von Richthofen, the "Red Baron" 's uncle) became the driving force behind the development of Montclair. The town was annexed by Denver in 1903. The land occupied by Lowry headquarters on 6th and Quebec was, in 1891, platted as Montclair Heights.

1887

Oct.31 - Fort Logan was founded in southwest Denver. The location was chosen by Gen. Phillip Sheridan. First called Fort Sheridan by the locals, it was officially named in honor of the civil war general John Alexander Logan. Fort Logan served as an auxiliary post to Lowry during W. W. II. It was decommissioned in 1946. It now serves as a national cemetery and mental health facility. (A Brief Hist. of Fort Logan, CMHI at Fort Logan)

1888

The military spirit first came to the area in the form of Jarvis Hall, named after George E. Jarvis of Philadelphia. The Episcopal military academy was built by Bishop John F. Spalding, (1828 -1902) bishop of Colorado. The hall was located between Quebec and Roslyn St, 9th and 11th Avenue. Jarvis Hall was part of a dream, along with a girl's school and a seminary, to create a university in the west to rival eastern schools. Unfortunately, it burned to the ground in 1901 and was abandoned. (Ref. Richthofen's Montclair, a pioneer Denver suburb by Thomas J. Noel)

1890

Ladies College, later Colorado Women's College (Vassar of the West) was established. Treat Hall, located at 16th and Quebec, is still standing and was declared a Denver landmark in 1975. (Ref. Lowry History File)

1891

The Stanley School at 13th and Quebec was built. The students were asked to name the school. They chose Henry Morton Stanley (born John Rowland, 1841-1904) journalist, famous African explorer and originator of the phrase "Dr. Livingston I Presume". The name was later changed to The Stanley British School. It is currently on the Lowry campus

1893

The United States Army Signal Corps established a War Balloon Company at Fort Riley, Kansas, at that time home of the Signal Corps. In 1894 another war balloon company was established at Fort Logan, Colorado. A French balloon was purchased for Fort Logan, the General Myer. When the balloon became unserviceable, another was made by Sgt. Ivy Baldwin(CAHOF), at the fort and named "Santiago" (Bond Photo.0006[1]) It saw limited service in Cuba in the Spanish-American War as a captive balloon.

1894

Dec.1 – Francis Brown Lowry was born in Denver. He attended Manuel H.S.

1903

Dec.17 – Wilbur Wright (1867-1912) and Orville Wright, (1871-1948) bicycle makers from Dayton Ohio, flew a plane (Wright Flyer I) at 10:30 AM. It flew 120 feet in 12 seconds at a speed of 6-8 mph. Orville was the pilot. Location – Kill Devil Hills, N.C. (Bond Photo.ZP-013)

1 Bond Photos are available at Photo Archives, Room 218, Wings Over the Rockies Museum.

1904

July 4 – The Agnes (Phipps) Memorial Sanatorium was opened at 6th and Quebec for the treatment of patients with early stage tuberculosis. At one time it held close to 300 patients. Due to the changes in treatment regimens, it closed in 1931-32. (Bond Photo. – BB-152-153)

1907

The Aeronautical Division, Signal Corps, 1st Army Air Unit was established with B/Gen. James Allen as Chief Signal Corps Officer and Capt. Charles Chandler, OIC, Aerodivision.

The Conclusion of the Air Corps Story

Air Force Magazine, May 1997, printed an article entitled, "The Nation's Air Arm and its Early Leaders."

The Aeronautical Division, U.S. Signal Corps was organized on Aug. 1, l907 and ceased to exist on July 18, 1914.

The Aviation Section, U.S. Signal Corps was organized on July 18, 1914 and ceased to exist on May 24, 1918.

The Air Service was organized on May 24, 1918, and ceased to exist on July 2, 1926.

The Air Corps was organized on July 2, 1926, and ceased to exist on Sept. 18, 1947. The Air Corps became a subordinate element of the Army Air Forces June 20, 1941. Since the Air Corps had been established by statute in 1926, its disestablishment required an act of Congress, which did not take place until 1947. Between March 9, 1942, and Sept. 18, 1947, the Air Corps continued to exist as a combatant arm of the Army, and personnel of the Army Air Forces were still assigned to the Air Corps.

The Army Air Forces were organized on June 20, 1941, and ceased to exist on Sept. 18, 1947. The USAF was created on Sept. 18,1947.

1908

Sept. 3 – Wright Model A demonstrated at Ft. Myer, VA.

1909

Aug. 2 – Wright Model B (flown by Orville, on board LT. Lahm) was accepted by the Signal Corps. It becomes the 1st military plane in the world, birthday of the Army Air Force.

1910

Feb. 1,2,3 – Louis Paulhan (1883-1963) was born in Pezenas, Herault, France. After creating a reputation for flying and setting world records in Europe, he came to America to compete in air shows. He brought several Bleriot and Farman III aircraft with him. In January 1910, he competed in an air show in Los Angeles, where he set a world record for altitude (4,164 feet) and won a trophy for endurance flight (1 hr., 49min.) He then set another altitude record in Salt Lake City and came to Denver arriving on Feb. 1st and became the first person to fly an aircraft in Colorado. He performed in a Farman III on Feb.1, 2, 3 in Overland Park to a large and enthusiastic audience. On Feb.3, he crashed into a fence injuring several bystanders. He was unharmed. The Denver Post reported that he avoided injuring others due to his flying skills. He was called "King of the Skies" (Denver Post – Feb, 2, 3, 4, 1910) (Bond Photo. D-193A) to build flying machines and fly. Quite a few attempted it. Only a few succeeded. On July 22nd, 1910, W.L. Marr and E. Linn Mathewson flew a biplane at the aerodrome on Monaco Blvd. in Park Hill. It flew for 100 yards at a height of 20 ft. It was the first flight of a Colorado built plane.

Marr left for Texas and Mathewson was joined by George W. Thompson (CAHOF 1969) and George Van Arsdale (both aeronauts and inventors) to form the Mathewson Aeroplane Co. (Denver Post Jul.22,1910, Howard L. Scamehorn, "First 50 years of Flight in Colorado," U. of Co. Bul. 2, History Series 1961) Thompson was elected into the Colo. Aviation Hall of Fame in 1969.

Nov.15 – A Wright team consisting of Arch Hoxsey, Walter Brookins and Ralph Johnstone arrives in Denver to put on a flying exhibition at Overland Park. Amongst the three, there were several world flying records and they all were considered the most skillful, the most daring and the most courageous of the "Birdmen". The city responded with even more enthusiasm. (Denver Post, Nov.14, 15, 16, 17, 18.)

Nov.17 – Ralph Johnstone was killed in a flying accident at Overland, the cause of which was never fully established. He was the first (of many) Americans to die in an aircraft accident. (Denver Post, Nov.18, 1910)

1911

The Mathewson Aeroplane Co. set up shop at the Sable Motor Speedway (6 miles east of Denver) and built the Mathewson #2. George Thompson became the west's most famous early aviator.

1917

Mar.28 – The first Air Force Photo. School was established at Langley Field, Va.

Sept. 3 – F.B. Lowry graduated from Officers Training School, Fort Ridge, Va. as a Photo Aerial Observer.

1918

Sept.17 – 1st LT. John Harold "Buck" Buckley was killed in France. Flying in formation, he hit another allied plane. Both planes and pilots were lost. Buckley was born in Longmont, Co.

Sept.26 – 2nd LT. Francis B. Lowry was killed while photographing for the Meuse Argonne Offensive near Crepion, France. The pilot was Asher Kelty of Rice Lake, MI. Their plane (a Salmson A2A) was hit by antiaircraft fire. It was their 33rd mission. Both were later awarded the Distinguished Service Cross by General Order 21, US Army. (Bond Photo. D-153 and 154)

Dec.12 – A JN-4 (Jenny) was released from the Dirigible C-10 at 2500 ft. The plane landed safely. This was a first.

1919

Denver's first flying field opened at 2600 Oneida St. It was owned by I. B. Humphries. The location was near that of the future Stapleton Airport. For more on early airports in northeast Denver, see pages 11 and 12.

1920

Jun.4 – Airplane Pilot rating replaced Military Aviator (created in 5/27/12)

1921

Sep. – Lt. Lowry's remains were returned to Denver. Internment was at the Fairmount Cemetery.

1922

Army Photo. School established by the Air service at Chanute Field, Ill. (Bond Photo.C-02)

1923

Jun.26 – 120th Obs. SQDN.,45th Division Air Service, Colorado National Guard was mustered in at the Colorado N.G. Armory, 1321 Acoma St. Denver. The commanding officer was Carl Milliken. The unit consisted of 8 officers and 20 enlisted. Milliken was also the Colorado Secretary of State. Due to his lack of flying experience, he was soon replaced by William H. Dayton. At that time, there were no flying facilities or equipment. An airfield was obtained on 3/1924 at 38th Ave. and Dahlia St. On 4/7/1924 it was named Lowry Field and in May planes arrived.

Sep.4 – The first flight of the US Navy rigid frame dirigible was the first Navy airship to use helium, the USS Shenandoah. She flew across America. She served until Sep.3,1925 when caught in a storm, she was destroyed.

1924

Apr.7 – The airfield at 38th Ave. and Dahlia St. was named Lowry Field in honor of LT. Francis B. Lowry by the Adj. General's Office, Denver, CO. General Orders # 8. The federal government provided 2 hangars and by May 24, 5 Curtiss JNSE (Jenny) arrived by train from Duncan Field, San Antonio, Texas, unassembled. On June 27, Sgt. F. Kearns was the first to fly from Lowry. He circled the field at 70 MPH. (Ref – Colo. Forgotten Air Base. Frank Harper, Colorado Heritage, Autumn, 1994.)
The following is a list (perhaps not complete) of aircraft arriving at Lowry Field early in its existence:5 JNSE – Sep.24, 1924 (Bond Photo. AA1-1962), Douglas O-2C – Sep, 1926 (Bond Photo. 226), a BT-1 – 1926 (a variant of O-2C), 4 Consolidated PT-1 – May 27, 1927 (Bond Photo. AA1-278), 2 Consolidated O-17 – 1930 (Bond Photo. AA1-230A), Douglas O-38 – 1933, (Bond Photo. AA1-233), Thomas Morse O-19E – 1935 (Bond Photo. AA1-231).

1925

Alexander Aircraft Co. started in Englewood, CO. by J. Don and Don M. Alexander (CAHOF -1970) A great story. (Alexander Eaglerock, Col John A. deVries, Century One Press, 1985)

1926

Jan.7 – First Flight of an Alexander Eaglerock aircraft. **Oct.** – Richard Byrd in a Fokker Trimotor visited Denver, (Bond Photo. AA5-02).

1927

Aug.31 – After completing his historic transatlantic flight in May, Charles Lindbergh went on a nationwide tour. He arrived in Denver from Omaha on Aug. 31 to a huge adoring crowd. He landed at Lowry Field in the "Spirit of St. Louis", followed by a city tour accompanied by the Governor and the Mayor. Cheering admirers lined the route of the motorcade.

During his visit, Lindbergh reportedly commented that Lowry Field was one of the finest equipped and maintained single unit fields in the United States. He left for Pierre, SD the next day. The impact Lindbergh had on America and the western world cannot be overestimated. In the year following the flight, he visited all 48 states. In 1927, one fourth of Americans (30 million) came to see the quiet, shy farm boy from Little Falls, Minnesota and the "Spirit." Aircraft and pilot's licenses increased dramatically. In 1926, there were 5,782 airline passengers. In 1929 the number had increased to 173,405 (Bond Photo. D-145) (Ref: Lowry Air Force Base, Ballard, Bond, Paxton, page 11)

1928

Apr.16 - Lindbergh returned during 1928 for a second visit in a B-IX Brougham (sister ship of the "Spirit of St. Louis", named the "Spirit of Unrest" in California) (Bond Photo. A1- 36A) He flew in unannounced with two passengers from the Grand Canyon on a "vacation trip". Lindbergh spent the night at Octave Chanute's home. When he attempted to depart, he found the runway at Lowry Field too short for his passenger load. He flew solo to the Alexander Airfield, (approx. Hampden and I-25, today) his passengers arriving separately.

Oct.17 – Denver Municipal Airport was dedicated, Mayor Benjamin F. Stapleton (Denver major, 1923-31 and 1935-47) presiding.

39.77 North / 104.93 West (Northeast of Downtown Denver, CO)

A circa 1924 aerial view of buildings & hangars at the original Lowry Field.

A Brief Review of Early Airports in Northeast Denver

Colorado's interest in the flying machine goes back to the formation of the Aero club of Colorado in 1915 and its part in the birth of the Signal Corps branch of the Colo. National Guard (Denver Post - 12/11/16) and to returning veterans of WW I.   Although there were various fields before used to fly and land planes, the first commercial airfield in East Denver was Humphries Field started in 1919. Fields included some or all of the following: hangars, repair shops, a plane manufacturing company or used plane dealerships, flying lessons, and mail and passenger service. Below are listed significant airports and locations that helped bring Colo. into the age of flight.

26th and Oneida

Humphries Field - 1919-1922. I. B. Humphries (CAHOF 1969) was the Curtiss-Wright dealer and owned the Curtiss-Humphries Airplane Co. in Denver. The field was also known as the East Denver Aerodrome. Don Hogan Airfield - 1925, also known as Colorado Airways Aerodrome. The company that ran the airport was Colo. Airways Inc., founded by Tony Joseph. It was the location of the first transcontinental air mail thru Denver in 1926. Humphries elected to CO. Aviation Hall of Fame in 1969. Higley Field - 1934. Walter Higley bought the airport from Tony Joseph and established the 1st organized flying school in Colo.
 Civil Air Patrol Airport - 1942
 Closed – 1946

38th and Dahlia

It was selected by Colorado National Guard for a training field 1-3/1924 The Denver City Council approved a 10-year lease for the land from the Evans Investment Co. 3/31/1924.

Land to be subleased to the state
(Rocky Mtn. News - 4/1/1924)
The field was named for F. B. Lowry 4/7/1924, Planes (Jenny) arrived on 5/24, by truck, unassembled.
1st flight – 6/24, pilot Sgt. Daniel F. Kearns (CAHOF 1970), Air Show – 8/24. Construction approved for COANG hangar at Denver Municipal Airport 3/36 Guard moved to Muni. later in 1936.
The name Lowry moved to 6th and Quebec in 1938.
Field bought by Harry Combs (CAHOF 1998) in1939. Known as Combs Airpark home of Mountain States Aviation and Combs Aircraft Corps. Closed - 1/14/1949

48th and Dahlia

Denver Union Airport / Rocky Mtn. Airport -1928 Both names seemed to be used for this location early in its existence - 1928.
Curtiss-Wright Airport – 1929, the airplane company bought the field and changed the name. During the depression the company closed the field in 1931.
Frank Van Dersarl (CAHOF 1969) ran the location for a short while but closed.
Park Hill Airport - 1935-1941. Ray Wilson (CAHOF 1970) a former employee bought the field and started a flying school.
Hayden Field – 1941 (Harry Combs involved) later it became
Vest Field owned by Don Vest. Closed - 1953

8100 E 32nd Ave.

Denver Municipal Airport - opened Oct. 17,1929
Stapleton Airport - Aug. 25, 1944, named in honor of former mayor
Stapleton International Airport - Oct.16, 1964. Closed - Feb. 1995.
Note - The 1926 Denver City Directory lists Rocky Mtn. Air Lines at 1827 Bellaire under Air Ports. No other reference was found.

CAHOF – Colo. Aviation Hall of Fame. A complete list of honorees is available at the Colo. Aviation Hist. Soc. Headquarters located at the Wings Museum. (colahs.org)

PAULHAN'S FLIGHTS END WHEN AIRSHIP SWEEPS INTO CROWD AND IS WRECKED

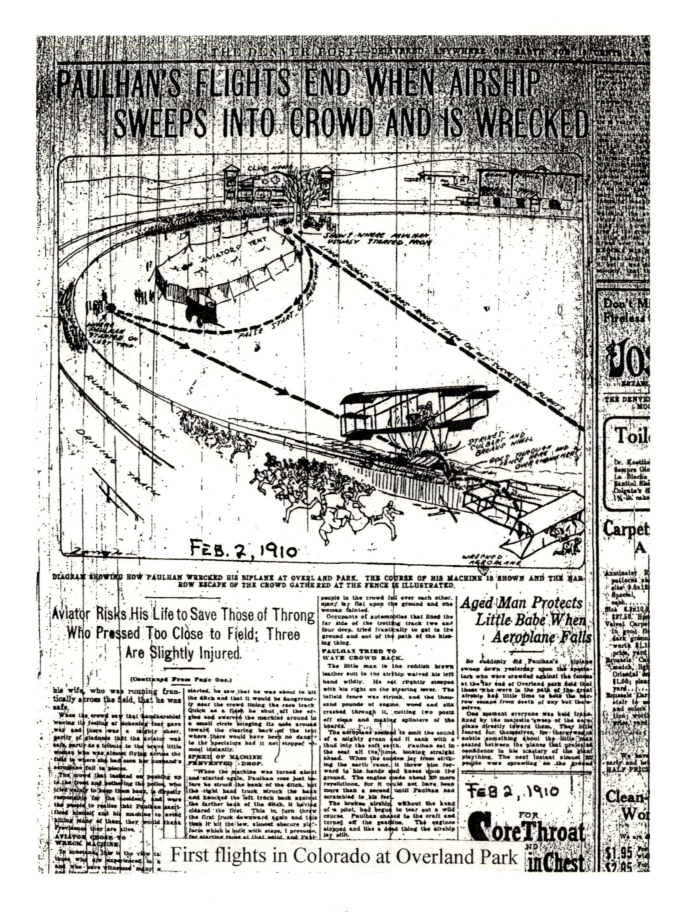

FEB. 2, 1910

DIAGRAM SHOWING HOW PAULHAN WRECKED HIS BIPLANE AT OVERLAND PARK. THE COURSE OF HIS MACHINE IS SHOWN AND THE NARROW ESCAPE OF THE CROWD GATHERED AT THE FENCE IS ILLUSTRATED.

Aviator Risks His Life to Save Those of Throng Who Pressed Too Close to Field; Three Are Slightly Injured.

(Continued From Page One.)

his wife, who was running frantically across the field, that he was safe.

When the crowd saw that handkerchief waving its feeling of sickening fear gave way and there was a mighty cheer, partly of gladness that the aviator was safe, partly as a tribute to the brave little woman who was almost flying across the field to where she had seen her husband's aeroplane fall to pieces.

The crowd that insisted on pushing up to the front and bothering the police, who tried vainly to keep them back, is directly responsible for the accident, and were the people to realize that Paulhan sacrificed himself and his machine to avoid killing many of them, they would thank Providence they are alive.

AVIATOR CHOSE TO WRECK MACHINE

In substance this is the view of those who are experienced in and who have witnessed many

started, he saw that he was about to hit the ditch and that it would be dangerously near the crowd lining the race track. Quick as a flash he shut off the engine and swerved the machine around in a small circle bringing its nose around toward the clearing back of the tent where there would have been no danger to the spectators had it not stopped almost instantly.

SPEED OF MACHINE PREVENTED DROP.

"When the machine was turned about and started again, Paulhan rose just before he struck the bank of the ditch, but the right hand truck struck the bank and knocked the left track back against the farther bank of the ditch, it having cleared the first. This in turn threw the first truck downward again and this time it hit the low, almost obscure platform which is built with steps, and presumably for starting races at that point and Paul-

people in the crowd fell over each other, many lay flat upon the ground and one woman fainted.

Occupants of automobiles that lined the far side of the trotting track two and four deep, tried frantically to get in the ground and out of the path of the hissing thing.

PAULHAN TRIED TO WAVE CROWD BACK.

The little man in the reddish brown leather suit in the airship waived his left hand with his right on the steering lever. The infield fence was struck, and the thousand pounds of engine, wood and silk crashed through it, cutting two posts off clean and making splinters of the boards.

The aeroplane seemed to emit the sound of a mighty groan and it sank with a thud into the soft earth. Paulhan sat in the seat all the time, looking straight ahead. When the sudden jar from striking the earth came, it threw him forward to his hands and knees upon the ground. The engine made about 200 revolutions, for it could not have been more than a second until Paulhan had scrambled to his feet.

The broken airship without the hand of a pilot, had begun to tear out a wild course. Paulhan chased the craft and turned off the gasoline. The engines stopped and like a dead thing the airship lay still.

Aged Man Protects Little Babe When Aeroplane Falls

So suddenly did Paulhan's biplane swoop down yesterday upon the spectators who were crowded against the fence at the far end of Overland park that those who were in the path of the great airship had little time to hold the narrow escape from death of any but themselves.

One moment everyone was held transfixed by the majestic sweep of the aeroplane directly toward them. They little feared for themselves, for there was a subtle something about the little man seated between the planes that projected confidence in his mastery of the giant plaything. The next instant almost 500 people were sprawling on the ground

FEB 2, 1910

First flights in Colorado at Overland Park

Chapter 2

1931 to 1940

1932

July – The Agnes (Phipps) Memorial Sanatorium closed. Originally opened in July, 1904, it was built for 80 to 150 patients, later increased to possibly 300. It had served during the time when Colorado was the mecca of open air treatment for tuberculosis. Many Coloradoans, famous and not famous in the state's history, immigrated to be cured of the "White Plague." Treatment regimens changed and the occupancy dwindled. However, more history was in store for the hospital complex and grounds.

1933

Apr.4 – The U.S.S. Akron(ZRS-4), a helium filled, rigid frame airship, commissioned in Oct.22, 1931, crashed off the New Jersey coast in a storm with the loss of 72 out of a crew of 75. Included in the loss was Rear Admiral William A. Moffett, Chief of the Navy's Bureau of Aeronautics. Among the Akron's duties, it served as a "flying aircraft carrier", launching and recovering F9C Sparrow Hawk planes. (Bond Photo – AA1-154A) The Akron had no life boats or life jackets.

1934

The Technical Training School at Chanute Field (Rantoul, Ill.) was declared inadequate by the army to meet the ever expanding needs of the air service. Buildings and classrooms were old and crowded. Weather was unfavorable for photography. The prospect of a bombing range was dim.

A committee was formed with M/Gen. Barton K. Yount (1884-1949) as the head of a search for a replacement. Yount visited 86 sites. The citizens of Denver, realizing the economic advantage of having a service facility in Denver, began to react. On March 14th, The Rocky Mountain News published an article "Fair Weather Fliers" and suggested Denver needed to convince the army to come to Denver. Stanley T. Wallbank, president of the Chamber of Commerce began a three - year campaign to bring the army to Denver. This included approval of a bond issue and purchase of land for the base. On Dec 9,1937 the City purchased the now vacant Agnes Memorial Sanatorium and its grounds from Lawrence C. Phipps for $200,000 and the erasure of back taxes. Efforts were also in progress to buy land southeast of Denver for a bombing range. The Army eventually obtained 880 acres for Lowry, 960 for the auxiliary field (Buckley) and 64,000 acres for the bombing range. (Office of History Lowry Training Center, Men for a Mechanized Army Part 1, pages 1 thru 19)

1935

Feb.12 – The U.S.S. Macon (ZRS-5), a helium filled rigid airship, sister of the U.S.S. Akron, damaged in a storm was lost off the Big Sur Coast, CA. It was commissioned in June 1933 and served as an observation ship and a flying aircraft carrier. All but two crewmembers were saved since now it was equipped with life jackets and life rafts.

Mar.1 – Air Force General Headquarters was created to control Tactical Air Operations   **1936**
Oct. – A Bombsight Maintenance Course was initiated at Chanute.

1937

16

Aug.27 – After a lengthy struggle with Illinois congressmen, a compromise was reached on March 1937, allowing the Denver Branch to begin photo and armament schools while Chanute retained command. Also on Aug.27th President Roosevelt signed the Army Housing Bill containing the Denver school provisions.

Sept. 1 – Capt. Harold D. Stetson (Army Quartermaster Corps) was transferred from Fort Logan to supervise the conversion of the existing buildings of the vacant sanatorium.

Oct. 1 – The flag was raised at the Denver Branch making it an active army post. This date became the official anniversary date of the base. Almost immediately conversion of the sanatorium buildings began, the WPA (Works Progress Administration) supplying the labor. The buildings were numbered in the # 250 series (first general order issued by Stetson). Also in October M/SGT Grover B. Gilbert was transferred by Chanute Field Special Order 222, to proceed to Denver and establish a photo school.

1938

Feb.7 – Lt. Col. Junius W. Jones (1890 -1977) became the first commander of the Denver Branch.

Feb.12 – The120[th] Observation Squadron, Colorado Air National Guard moved to the Denver Municipal Airport. National Guard post opened an engineering office and an air corps supply office located in the west half of the hangar leased from the state. Also on this date staff and students of the technical schools, 300 strong, arrived at Denver's Union Station.

Feb.26 – U.S. Army activates the Denver Branch, Air Corps Tech. Training School.

Feb.28 – Photo and armament instructions began and the first bombing and air machine gun practice began on the newly acquired bombing range.

Mar.2 – Secretary of War, Harry H. Wooding, upon the recommendation of Chief of Staff Gen. Malin Craig, selected the name Lowry Field for the new base. Also in March first new additions are added. Old hangars from the airfield at 38th and Dahlia were erected at the new Lowry along with other additional buildings.

Lowry Airman May 20th, 1983

"It all started Oct 1, 1937 and construction began three days later. Oddly enough, the deed for the sanatorium property did not pass into the hands of the US Army until Dec. 8, 1937. Also in December the War Dept. announced that the Denver Branch, Air Corps Tech. School would be named Lowry Field after Lt. Francis Brown Lowry, the first Denver aviator (actually aerial observer) killed in action during World War I. This change, however, did not take place until March 21, 1983 after a Colorado Air National Guard Field with the same name had been deactivated.

On the morning of Feb. 12, 1938, a troop train carrying the first 300 of the hundreds of thousands of students who would train at the new field arrived from Chanute Field to the Denver facility. The new students held their first classes on Feb. 28, 1938.

In the mean time the Army Corps of Engineers formally accepted the field on March 26, 1938. For all practical purposes the USAF Simpson Historical Research Center recognizes this date as the birth date of Lowry Air Force Base." Readers will note that this is a different date than the one listed on page 17. As occasionally happens, history will give you a choice.

Apr.4 – The first completed runway (unpaved) was christened when Col. Jones and Capt. Stetson landed a 5- ton attack plane (probably a Northrup A-17) there. This was the N-S runway. Jones declared the field in perfect condition (Denver Post April 4, 1938). Stetson announced the pouring of cement for the first hangar, #402, was about to begin and work was progressing on runways at the auxiliary field (Buckley).

Through 1938 aircraft assigned to Lowry continued to arrive. On March 9 the Denver Post announced the arrival of five B-18s which would be joined by a P-35, an A-17 and a B-6, already there. These and others were housed at the Denver Muni. Airport, awaiting sufficient runways and hangars at Lowry. Bombing and machine gun training started on Feb. 28 with planes flown from Denver Muni. to the auxiliary field, armed and then flown to the bombing range (Denver Post March 10, 1938). On June 30, however, nine aircraft were ferried from Denver Muni. to Lowry Field. (Pursuit of Excellence, Levy and Scanlon)

June.29 – First photography class graduated from Lowry.

July.1 – Col. Jacob H. Rudolf became commanding officer.

Aug.13 – The Army began a four year $3.5 million program of new construction at Lowry.

Oct.10 – Lowry Field began instructions in the clerical school.

Nov. – Hangar #1 (Bldg. 402) construction began and was completed in Aug.,1939. Officer/NCO Quarters (on Quebec St,) and the Quartermaster Building (#358) were under construction.

1939 - Tent City was created in response to a large influx of servicemen.

The exact date of its creation is unknown. The best guess is spring of 1939. (news clippings with photos dated Aug. 25, and Sep 25 exist) (Bond Photo.BB-289). At its peak it accommodated 600 servicemen. It was closed Oct. 17, 1940, being replaced by Bldg. #349. It probably remained empty until 1941 when it was removed to make way for Bldg.477, a mess hall.

Aug. – WAC barracks Series 400 by 6th Ave. gate construction began.

Sep. – Construction of brick Bldg.349 began. The building often referred to as "Buckingham Palace" and occasionally as the "Anthill" when completed (Oct. 7, 1940) was to become the largest dormitory in the U.S. Armed Forces.

Dec. – Paving of the north-south runway was completed.

Dec.13 – During 1938 and 1939 there were planes in and out of Lowry Field for convenience and for training. However, Lowry became a flying post of the Army Air Corps on December 13th 1939. On that date Col. Joseph H. Rudolf, flying a B-18 Bolo, led the first armada of 13 planes on a thirty block flight from the Municipal Airport to bring in the first plane on Lowry Field's first concrete runway, and to nest in Lowry's first new hangar (Lowry Air Force Base Flight Operations, A Chronology). The remaining 12 planes belonging to the station were ferried in the next day.

1940

In January, Lowry Field housed 44 officers and 1350 enlisted men. There were 27 aircraft including the following – 9 B-18s, 7 P-35s, 6 A-19s, 2 P-36s (Bond Photo AA1-254), 1 BC-1, 1 O-46, and a large cargo plane.

Jun. – Construction of Hangar #2 (Bldg.401) was started and completed on April 17th 1941. Numbers for the hangars are confusing. They started out as noted in this chapter. Around the time that flying stopped (1966), the numbers were reversed. Bldg.401 became Hangar #1 and Bldg.402 became Hangar #2. They remain so to this day.

Jul.6 – 36th Bomber Squadron arrived at Lowry.

Jul.11 – 37th Bomber Squadron arrived. Both arrived from Barksdale, LA. B-24 crews were TDY for training purposes. Tent City housed some of both squadrons. Both departed May 29, 1941. B-18s from the 36th Bomber Squadron did reconnaissance and photography of Alaska and the Bering Sea, part of the 28th Composite Group, 1st Bomb Wing.

Jul.16 – Bombardier Instructor training began under the command of Capt. Frederick Anderson. The first class was composed of 20 cadets, most of whom were men who failed to complete aviator training. Eighteen graduated on Nov. 2. The second class started on Sept. 9, with 60 men and finished on Jan. 10 with 55. The third class of 60 started on Nov. 12 and finished on March 14, 1941 with 49. There was a fourth class for bombardiers, not instructors. The school closed in 1941 with graduates being transferred to Barksdale Field, LA., Ellington Field, Texas., Stockton, CA. and other bases. This school was to be the most unique and consequential school developed at Lowry. These instructors went on to teach others to be instructors, who taught others and so on. Between 7/40 and 1/45 the Army Air Corps trained 45,000 bombardiers. Lowry played a significant role in that process. (Michael F. Hamrick, History of Bombardier)

Sep.13 – Chaplaincy was activated at Lowry in a tent near the 6th Ave. gate. Worship services were held in Bldg. 365 (a hangar used as ½ gym, ¼ mess hall and ¼ chapel)

Oct. – 21st School Squadron activated.

Nov.18 – Start of Spanish language school for all officers.

Nov.27 – WPA began building a military road connecting Aux. Field (Buckley) and Lowry along 6th Ave. paralleling the railroad, 30 feet wide with oiled surface. The cost was $339,891.

Late 1940 – Lowry Railroad became operational.

Moving Day on the Plains.

AIR SCHOOL BEGINS BOMBING AND NOBODY IS DISTURBED

Fears of Residents Near Target Range Calmed as

Live Remarks by

MARCH 1, 1938

THE POST PHONE—MAIN 2121

AIR SCHOOL WILL START DAILY BOMBING PRACTICE ON MONDAY

Four or Five Planes Will Be Used and Hundred-Pound Missiles Dropped at First; Excavations Started for Underground Magazines.

Daily aerial bombing and machine gun practice will start Monday at the army air corps technical school, Capt. Herbert W. Anderson, director of the armament division, announced Thursday.

Using four planes, and possibly five, fifteen students will start their practice at the range twelve miles east of Denver. Two fifty-foot bombing targets have been prepared and two 6x10-foot machine gun targets have been completed, Captain Anderson said.

All the bombs and machine guns will be loaded on the planes at the auxiliary field, and from there will be flown to the range.

POUNDERS TO BE USED FOR PRESENT.

"There will be no danger to anyone who stays away from the bombing range and it is doubtful if anyone living nearby will be bothered," Captain Anderson said. "It is hardly likely that the explosion will even be heard in Denver."

For the present daily practice, nothing larger than 100-pound bombs will be used, Captain Anderson said.

Excavations have been started at the auxiliary field for partly underground high explosive magazines, which when completed will have a capacity of 150,000 pounds of bombs. At present only a small supply is being kept at the field. Most of the machine gun ammunition is stored at the school in Denver.

FIELD BEING PUT IN SHAPE RAPIDLY.

Since class instruction began Feb. 21, bombing and machine gunning has been restricted to only a few days a week because of lack of facilities, both at the range and the auxiliary field.

The field is rounding into suitable shape rapidly, Captain Anderson said. Two of the five runways have been completed and are in use.

Arrival in Denver Wednesday afternoon of the large B-18 bomber, the largest plane to be stationed here permanently for the present, virtually completed the squadron of planes necessary for adequate instruction.

This large bomber from Chanute field was expected last week but was held at Pueblo since last Friday because of inclement weather and a flat tire.

CREW OF SIX USED ON BIG BOMBER.

The plane, the latest model Douglas, is the second largest bombing type in the army. It is twin-motored, has a speed of approximately 200 miles an hour, and is more than 100

24

Chapter 3

1941 to 1950

1941

The years 1940 to 1945 at Lowry were devoted to the buildup and participation in World War II. The effort was shown by a tremendous expansion of construction and personnel. The following is one example.

Graduates from Training Schools

1938 – 244
1939 – 615
1940 – 1,230
1941 – 6,144
1942 – 21,261
1943 – 56,000(40,000-Arm. School)
9/44 to 6/45 – 40,000

Although the maximum effort was on armament and photography, there were two programs unique to Lowry Field and therefore are worth noting, the Bombardier Instructor program and the Remote Control Turret Training.

Jan.6 – 120th Obs. Squadron, 45th Div. Colorado Nat. Guard was mobilized to active duty and transferred to Briggs Field, El Paso, TX. (probably from Denver Muni.)

Feb.1 – The need for clerical training in the AAC increased significantly. Since the course required no air time, Fort Logan became a sub post of Lowry. Clerical classes were transferred and began on March 3, thus making space for some 1300 more armament students at Lowry.

In February concrete runways were completed.

Feb.20 – NCO (encio) village construction was started, completed in July. The cost of rental was $23.50/mo. Plus utilities. (1200 series bldgs.)

Mar.3 – Aviation Cadet School, consisting of Aviation Photo. Lab. Commanders and Armament Officer classes began.

Mar.26 – The Army Air Corps formed the Technical Training Command at Chanute Air Base.

May – Catholic Mass was held in a hangar. The hangar shared with General Mess #2.

May2 - $625,000 was requested for the bombing range, runway paving and lighting.

May9 – 1st edition of the weekly newspaper Rev-Meter was published.

May21 – A brass cannon, a gift from Fort Logan, was dedicated. The cannon was placed in front of HQ. (Bldg. 254, old sanatorium).

May25 – 36th and 37th Bomber Squadrons, which had given support to the bombardier instructors school, departed for Oregon and North Pendleton.

Jun.19 – 5740 acres,6 miles east of Denver was purchased by the city of Denver and donated to the U.S. Army to be used as an auxiliary field for Lowry. The named was changed the following year to Buckley Field. (See Chapter 9)

USAF Development

Jun.20 – According to the Air Force Historical Research Agency, the Army Air Corps became a subordinate element of the Army

Air Force (AAF) on June 20, l941, when Lt. Gen. Henry H. Arnold assumed the title of chief of Army Air Forces. The new AAF was directly under the orders of the chief of staff of the Army, Gen. George C. Marshall. Arnold and Marshall agreed that the AAF would enjoy autonomy within the War Department until the end of the war, when the air arm would become a fully independent service. However, unlike the Army Air Forces, the Army Air Corps was originally established by an act of Congress and could only be disestablished by another statute, which did not take place until 1947. Until then, personnel of the Army Air Force were officially assigned to the Army Air Corps. The authors apologize for the confusion.

Jul.8 – Chapel #1, Bldg.27, (protestant) and Chapel #2, Bldg.482 started construction. (See chapter 8)

Jul.18 – Pilot Training for African American Cadets began at Tuskegee, Alabama.

Jul.22 – Theatre #1, Bldg. 353 was dedicated. The first film was "One Night in Rio" starring Alice Fay, Don Ameche and Carmen Miranda.

Nov. – Service Club #1, Bldg. 483 opened.

Nov.23 – Chapels dedicated. (See Chapter 8.)

Napoleon said "an army marches on its' stomach." In 1941, Lowry Field spent $90,000 a month on groceries.

Dec.18 – Following the Japanese attack on Pearl Harbor, Lowry Field conducted an all base drill to defend against an aerial attack. It was well done. It was announced that similar drills would be held monthly. (Rev-Meter, Dec. 20, 1941)

1942

Feb. – The Photo School moved into a new 3 story brick building (#380). The Armament School moved into Bldg. 381.

Mar.1 – 24 B-25s were transferred to Eglin Airfield, Florida under the command of Col. James Doolittle in preparation for a raid on Tokyo. The raid occurred on April 18th.

Mar.2 – The Red Cross building was dedicated. (Bldg. 259). Also on Mar.2, the Army Air Force became a subordinate but autonomous arm of the U. S. Army.

Mar.15 – WAAC (Women's Army Auxiliary Corps) was formed by Public Law 554. Many women volunteered to help the war effort. All branches of service had female components. Army – WAAC

Navy – Women in the Navy (Waves)

Marines – Women Marines

Coast Guard – Spars

WAFS – Women's Aux. Ferrying

WFTD – Women's Flying Training Det.

The last two were combined in 1943 to become WASPS –Women's Air Force Service Pilots. The army alone had 150,000 women during WWII.

May18 – Ground breaking at Buckley Field including 700 buildings, a railroad spur, runways, etc. (See Chapter 9)

May29 – Sulfanilamide was added to service men's first aid kits.

Jun.1 – Colorado National Bank Branch opened on Lowry in bldg. 355

Jun.4 – Flag Day Celebration

Jul. – More expansion done to meet the needs of a nation at war. Lowry 2 opened in the northeast corner of the post. Kelly Rd. built around the north end of the n-s runway. East-West streets numbered, some named after air corps dignitaries or for the building on that street. Armament School #2 began at Buckley Field. Eventually armament classes were divided between Lowry and Buckley. Also in July, the NCO club opened in building #600A, renovated, updated and with an expanded kitchen – (Rev-Meter 4/16/43)

Aug.18 – Lowry and Fort Logan went to a 3 shifts/day, with a seven - day work week.

Aug.24 – The 941st Q.M, Platoon (colored) was activated with Lt. Chamillio O. Dorosio in command. (Rev-Meter, Mar./1944) In August an all service drive to collect metal for the war effort swallowed up the brass cannon on front of H.Q. It was replaced by a wooden one painted brass. In August, armament training was divided between Lowry and Buckley. Armament for bombers was taught at Lowry, and fighter armament was located at Buckley.

Oct.9 – Garrison caps were banned

Oct. 30 – The Red Cross moved into Bldg. 260.

Dec.11 – Bob Hope and Company visited Lowry.

1943

Jan.28 – WAAC personnel arrived at Lowry for photo training as the 997th WAAC Training Detachment. Also in January the first black photo class began.

feature

Volunteers brave WWII skies

They never engaged in bombing raids or dogfights over war-torn Europe. They never flew within 3,000 miles of the combat zone. But they were dedicated pilots who flew dangerous missions to help America win the air war during World War II.

Thirty-eight of these fliers lost their lives without ever leaving the United States. Twenty-six met their deaths in plane crashes, some while towing targets for air-to-air gunnery and some during artillery practice. Another 11 died in training accidents (one died as a passenger).

These unusual aviation pioneers of the early 1940s were called "WASPs" for Women Air Force Service Pilots. They were the first women in history to be trained to fly military aircraft.

Some 25,000 women enthusiastically signed up to become WASP ferry pilots, but only 1,879 were accepted and 1,076 made it through the rigorous seven-week training course at Avenger Field, Sweet-water, Texas. After graduation, they flew every fighter and cargo aircraft the Army Air Force had during the war years.

Their emblem, featuring a little lady gremlin called "Fifinella," was designed for the WASPs by the late cartoonist and moviemaker Walt Disney.

The WASP was formed to supplement an inadequate supply of male pilots. They ferried new aircraft from factories to airfields, towed targets for gunnery practice and tested planes within the United States. They also served as pilots for navigation and bombardier students, towed gliders, and served as instrument and flight instructors for male pilots training for combat. Additionally, they were assigned to dangerous engineering flight testing, radio-controlled flying experiments, airline operation for military transport missions and simulated strafing runs. They did everything their male counterparts did short of going into combat.

They were not officially members of the military, but they served in uniform as part of the Army Air Force from September 1942 until December 1944. The women were hired under civil service regulations with an annual salary of $3,000-$250 monthly. They were given all the privileges of a commissioned officer in the rank of lieutenant. But they received no promotions, and there wasn't any chance of advancement. Government insurance and other routine benefits were also denied to them as civil servants.

There were more WASPs flying airplanes during World War II than there are women pilots in today's Army (314), Navy (76) and Air Force (274). (This total of 664 women in the Department of Defense was compiled during fiscal 1985. The Marine Corps does not train female pilots.)

"We checked out and flew domestic missions in everything from the smallest trainer aircraft to the largest bomber," said Bea "Falk" Haydu, 65, a former WASP who now lives in Riviera Beach, Fla. "We flew the hot pursuit fighters such as the P-51, P-40, P-47, P-38 and P-39. We also flew the Flying Fortress B-17 bomber, the B-24 Liberator and the Superfortress B-29.

"WASPs also checked out and piloted the jet fighter, which was just coming into its own at that time," added Haydu, who is also a past president of the WASP organization.

Haydu said the women received the same training as male cadets. Although acrobatic maneuvers weren't stressed, they did practice them. "Acrobatic maneuvers are useful in combat flying and the WASPs were not being trained for combat," said Haydu, who was in her early 20s when she became a WASP. "However, the flight training, ground school, physical education, Morse code, radio techniques, military drill and courtesies, barracks inspections and every other aspect of military training was the same as that given to the male cadets."

Some of the women had problems venturing into jobs previously held only by men. "Some men never accept[ed]," said Haydu. "Some commanders [didn't want] women would fly airplanes on the [...] and gave the women other thing[s] or only let them fly small aircraft [...] tried to belittle them.

"Some women couldn't hand[le them]selves diplomatically as they sho[uld] entering a man's world," said [...] "But I personally had no bad [experi]ences.

"In my generation, we did[n't have] women's lib," she continued. "In [...] we were simply lucky to fly a pl[ane in a] male-dominated field. A lot [of women] can't understand what was going [on in] those days. We felt fortunate to b[e allow]ed to do these things. It [was a] stroke of luck. We didn't fe[el we could] go out and do all the thing[s we] could do.

"Due to the experiment[al nature of] the program, the WASP [received no] recognition at the time," [Haydu said]. "The intervening 30-plus year[s history] has largely overlooked the [progress] we made toward winning the [air war in] World War II."

They wore military [uniforms] under military authority and [were bound] by the Uniform Code of Mil[itary Justice]. But they had to fight for m[any] years to get veterans benefit[s].

President Jimmy Carter [signed a bill] in 1977 giving former WASP[s veteran] status.

In his farewell addres[s to the last] class of women cadets, the [late Gen.] "Hap" Arnold, former chie[f of the] Army Air Forces, said: "I am [glad to be] here today and talk with [you] women who have been mak[ing] history. You, and all WASP[s, are] pioneers in a new field of [aviation].

"You and more than 5[00 of your] sisters have shown that [you can fly] wingtip to wingtip with [the men]," said Arnold. "If ever there [was ever in] anyone's mind that women c[an be] skillful pilots, the WASP ha[ve dispelled] that doubt..." (American F[orces] Service)

W.A.S.P.
WOMEN AIR FORCE SERVICE PILOTS WWII
Fifinella

The 'Fifinella' emblem that was created for the WASPs by the Walt Disney [Studios]

(Courtesy Photo)

WASP ferry pilot Bee (Falk) Haydu stands on the wing of trainer aircraft at Avenger Field, Sweetwater, Texas, during World War II.

Evolution of USAF Aircraft Insignia

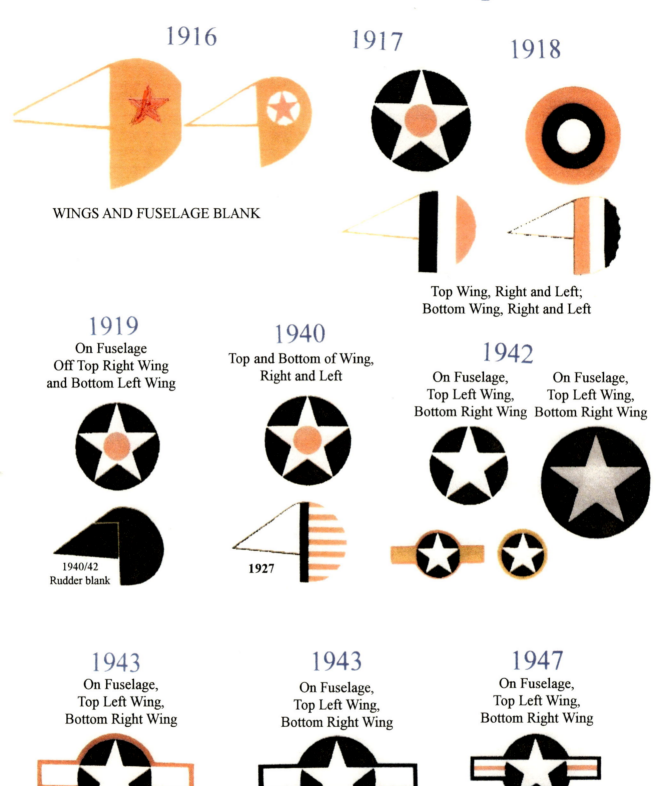

1916

WINGS AND FUSELAGE BLANK

1917

1918

Top Wing, Right and Left;
Bottom Wing, Right and Left

1919
On Fuselage
Off Top Right Wing
and Bottom Left Wing

1940/42
Rudder blank

1940
Top and Bottom of Wing,
Right and Left

1927

1942
On Fuselage,
Top Left Wing,
Bottom Right Wing

On Fuselage,
Top Left Wing,
Bottom Right Wing

1943
On Fuselage,
Top Left Wing,
Bottom Right Wing

1943
On Fuselage,
Top Left Wing,
Bottom Right Wing

1947
On Fuselage,
Top Left Wing,
Bottom Right Wing

Mar.1 – The Department began instructions for the B-29 "Super fortress. This included the B-29's Central Fire Control course. At that time, Lowry was the only facility in the air corps to offer the Central Fire Control course. The 3415th Training Command.

Mar4 – The 380th Bomb Group (B-24s) transferred to the Pacific

Apr.9 – A minstrel show was performed at Lowry. Because of it's popularity the show had repeat performances on base and also performed in downtown Denver.

Apr.23 – President Roosevelt visited Lowry which was part of his nationwide tour of service facilities. On April 24, the first WAAC photo class graduated 43 students.

May7 – The first edition of the Rev-Meter with a B-17 in the title was published .

Jun.1 – The Colorado National Bank Branch moved into its own building.

Jun.3 – Camp Bizerte opened on the northwest corner of the bombing range. It closed on October 11, 1943. During that time 20,000 men had received basic field training. In October, it moved to Lowry 2 for the winter in the class 26 area west of theatre #2. On June 4, the black Recreation Center opened.

Jul.7 – Flying Training Command and Technical Training Command were combined to form the Army Air Force Training Command located at Fort Worth, TX.   In July, the Red Dot was removed from aircraft roundels(stars) so not to be confused with the "Rising Sun" on Japanese aircraft. White rectangles and red boarder were also added.

Sep.30 – WAAC became WAC, Women's Army Corps. Ranks became similar to AAC(men).

WAC remained throughout W.W.II and continued until 1948, when the U.S.A.F. became a separate branch of the Arm Services. At that time, WAC became WAF (Women in the Air Force). WAF was disbanded in 1978 by the Women's Armed Forces Integration Act. 1978 was also the first year the Air Force Academy accepted women.

Oct.22 – Flight Engineers School transferred from Smoky Hill Army Air Field to Lowry.

1944

Mar.3 – A service club for black servicemen was opened in Bldg. 805. In March a black orchestra was formed, the musicians were from the 41st Technical School Squadron, and in March the Hotel de Gink (Bldg. 251) was closed.

Apr.1 – Black Turret Graduation occurred. Possibly named because of African-American Troops involved in the training.

Jun.2 – A plaque honoring Francis Brown Lowry was placed in front of the headquarters building. (Rev-Meter June 2, 1944)

Jul.4 – Lowry open House was held. During the war these were very popular. (long lines at the B-24)

Jul.24 – B-24 Copilot Training started. This was the first Lowry course for "pilot phase" training.

Aug.25 – "Little Fellow" insignia by Cpl. George Grimes was awarded

winner in the base insignia contest.

Also on Aug.25, 1944, the Denver Municipal Airport was renamed Stapleton Airport in honor of former Denver Mayor Ben Stapleton.

Sep.29 – Rev-Meter had B-29 in the headline, replacing the B-17.

Nov.27 – The Clerical School returned to Lowry from Fort Logan.

At the end of 1944, Lowry had 19,620 military and civilian personnel on the base.

1945

In the first quarter of 1945 the base population at Lowry began to reduce. Many areas in the services had sufficient trained personnel and the war in Europe was felt to be drawing to a close. Enlisted men on March 1st was at 16,379. By April 30, it had reduced to 11,898. Total military personnel went from 19,181 on March 1, to 14,749 on April 30th. Civilian personnel decreased by similar numbers.

Feb.19 – Armament courses changed from B-17 and B-24 to B-29s and B-32s. Armament classes in general reduced by ½ by the end of February. Contrary to the trend on base, Flight Engineer school enrollment increased. Another increase was in clerical training. The increase was mainly in female students.

Mar. – Lowry had 104 aircraft on base of which 72 were B-24s.

May.8 – V. E. Day

Midyear – Because of the increased production of B-29s and the AAF's concentration on war in the Pacific, more flying schools were needed. Lowry was chosen as one.

May16 – Flight Engineer School was transferred to Hondo Field, TX, to make room for the flight school.

May18 – The first of 42 B-29s arrived at Lowry under the command of Lt. Col. Anthony Perna.

Jul.20 – The 1st class (pilot, copilot, and flight engineer) of 80 crews began a 6- week course.

Aug.15 – V.J. Day: B-29 classes were never completed. All classes were terminated on Sept. 26. So ended Lowry's very short history as a pilot school.

Aug. – A B-29 modification center was located at Stapleton Airport. On Aug.26th, the Denver Post revealed that B-29s were being modified and repaired with a "Mickey" (electric bombsights) at the Continental Airlines Denver Modification Center. It was all very secret until the 26th. Photos show a B-29 parked on the ramp. Possibly, a M.A.D. is a Magnetic Anomaly Detection to improve night operations.

Sep.19 – As all student numbers decreased from 5,324 in October to 2,938 in December, there was a ten- fold increase in the Dept. of Clerical Instruction. At war's end, Lowry became a separation center. Classes also resumed a 5- day schedule and one shift per day.

1946

Jul.1 – Army Air Force Training Command became Air Training Command. Buckley Field was placed on inactive status at the end of the war and again became an auxiliary field for Lowry.

The newly formed Colorado Air National Guard (COANG) was granted a right-of-entry permit in Dec. 1946 and assumed responsibility for the site. (www.buckley.af.mil/library/factsheet)

1947

Jan.30 – Orville Wright died. Most of his (and Wilber's) last years were devoted to legal battles around patent rights with Glenn Curtiss and others. In 1947 the U. S. Navy assumed control and renamed Buckley Field, Naval Air Station-Denver(NAS-D)

Mar.21 – The War Department formed Strategic Air Command(SAC), Technical Air Command and the Air Defense Command.

Jul.1 – Army Air Force Day at Lowry Field.
Jul.15 – Air Intelligence School was transferred to Lowry from Keesler Field, Miss.
Jul.26 – President Harry S. Truman signed the National Security Act, forming a Dept. of Defense with separate Depts. of the Army, Navy and the Air Force.

Sep.18 – W. Stuart Symington was sworn in as Secretary of the Air Force. The following week, Gen. Carl Spaatz became chief of the USAF.

1948

Several changes came with the creation of the Air Force. Sometime late in 1947 or early in 1948, pursuit ships became fighters. P designation became F. On June 12th, WAC became WAF (Women in the Air Force) WAF was abolished in 1978 when they were fully integrated.
Jun.13 - Lowry field became Lowry Air Force Base.

Jun. – Operation Vittles (Berlin Airlift) began. It ended in Sept. 1949.

Jul.26 – President Harry S. Truman issued Executive Order 9981, abolishing segregation in the armed forces. Criticism and resistance was considerable both inside and outside the service. The Korean War helped make it a reality due to significant casualties in many units. It was six years (Sept, 1954) before the last colored unit was disbanded.

Sept. – An athletic field was established in front of Bldg.349.

Oct. – U.S.A.F. replaced U.S. Army on the roof of Hangar #401. Warehouse #594 burned sometime after 1948. The second floor on Hangar #402 was built shortly after 1948.

1949

Jan.3 – Operation Hayride (also Haylift, Snowbound) began. Eighteen snowstorms in 27 days hit the Rocky Mountains and upper great plains region in Dec., '48 and Jan.'49, dropping temperatures to 40 below zero, blocking roads and railroads, covering the ground with so much snow that hundreds of thousands of livestock were threatened with starvation. The 2151st Rescue Unit at Lowry began to airdrop food and medicine to the stranded. For the next ten days the unit flew C-47s, C-82s, L-5s and H-5s over Colorado, Wyoming and Nebraska. Eventually, additional help was needed. The operation ended on March 15. (Daniel L. Haulman, USAF Humanitarian Airlift Ops., 1947-1994 Wash. D.C., Air Force History and Museum Program 1998) (Bond Photos. L007A)

May – Sunset Village (#1120-1181 was built. The Quebec and 6th Ave. entrance was paved.

Jun.24 – Bombs replaced cannons in front of the HQ. building.

Dec. – AF Chief of Staff Hoyt S.Vandenberg recalled Lt. Gen. Hubert R. Harmon to head the Office of Special Assist for "Air Force Academy Matters."

1950

Brick Housing was built at Quebec St. and 11ᵗʰ Ave.

Jun.17 – Lowry began a 6- day training week to support manpower requirements for the Korean War.

Note: Building 1 to 10, officer's qtrs. 1943-1949

Building 201 to 210, NCOs

Building 1 to 10, 201 to 210, became all officers qtrs. in 1955

Some readers may be offended by the use of the terms black, colored or negro. For the sake of authenticity, we have used the Official Army designation for those unit during their existence.

Lowry Field -METER

D — Denver, Colorado — January 29, 1943   No. 37

Lowry WAACs Arrive, to Begin Training Monday

(Continued from page 1)

military lines. Officials at the department of photography said the course the corps members will study will be the same as those studied by enlisted men. Length of instruction will be 12 weeks.

Following their graduation from the photo school, the WAAC's, it was reported, would be assigned lab operations and technical work in the Army Air Forces.

Such duties, authorities said, though they will be of the noncombatant type, as in other WAAC work, will be either in this country or overseas.

First Lt. Johnston, the squadron commander of the detachment, is from Union, W. Va. She is a graduate with an A.B. degree from Marshall College in that state. In civilian life she was a school teacher in Union. She was one of the first women to join the corps, when its organization and policies were under experiment in July, 1942, at Des Moines.

Second Lt. Starbuck, the squadron adjutant, is a native of Brighton, Colo. Following her schooling there, she entered Loretto Heights College in Denver and was graduated in 1940. She joined the WAAC's in July, 1942, and is another veteran of the corps.

The question of saluting WAAC officers, now in the minds of military personnel here, was answered at post headquarters. Officials said that it would be a post policy and a matter of common military courtesy for both officers and enlisted men to salute WAAC officers and render them other courtesies afforded a commissioned officer. A similar policy applies to Army nurses.

Aiding Lts. Johnston and Starbuck in the administration of the WAAC detachment are 1st Sgt. Mary G. Redden, from Tallassee, Ala.; Supply Sgt. Helen Darak, Bridgeport, Conn., and Detachment Clerk Cpl. Frances Lee, Eutaw, Ala.

At present there are three WAAC training centers. These are, in addition to Des Moines, at Daytona Beach, Fla., and at Fort Oglethorpe, Ga.

Buy a bond. It's insurance for you and the U. S.!

Lowry Greets First Women Soldiers As WAACs Arrive for Photo School

ALL COURTESIES WILL BE EXTENDED to WAAC officers, headquarters announced this week, and a Lowry private carries out his orders when he meets Lt. Dorothy L. Starbuck, adjutant for the new WAAC detachment which arrived this week.

Group to Start Classes Monday; Quarters Ready

Technical training at Lowry Field entered a new phase with the arrival early yesterday of the first detachment of WAAC's from Des Moines, Iowa, for enrollment and training in the department of photography.

Preparations have been made at the photo school, officers there said, to start the first WAAC classes Monday.

Everything in Readiness

The vanguard of the Women's Army Auxiliary Corps entered the field last week, when 1st Lt. Elizabeth Johnston, commanding officer of the group, and 2nd Lt. Dorothy L. Starbuck, squadron adjutant, came to Lowry with three assistants to make final preparations for the arrival of the bulk of the corps now at Lowry.

Quarters for the detachment, the only women's organization, exclusive of the Army Nurse Corps, authorized to serve with the Army, will be an area previously occupied by the 25th School Squadron, across from the post office.

Field officials said the WAAC's—who, following their schooling at the Des Moines training center, are sent to serve at military installations in this country or abroad—would come to the field in greater numbers in future months.

The move is in line with the War Department's policy of replacing soldiers with WAAC's or civilian employes, thus making the soldiers available for more active assignments.

Assigned to Headquarters

While here the WAAC detachment will be attached temporarily to Hqs. & Hqs. Squadron, AFTS, commanded by Capt. John R. Peterson. The detachment is at present on detached service from Des Moines, where it will report for future assignments following its schooling here.

As at Des Moines, the training given the WAAC's at Lowry will be along

A Highly Significant 'First'

LOWRY'S FIRST NEGRO PHOTO GRADUATES will receive diplomas Saturday, signifying successful completion of an intensive Army Air Forces Technical Training Command photography course. Shown in the upper photo are students who took the Advanced Laboratory course. From left to right they are, top row, Staff Sgt. Harold J. Beaulieu, Cpl. Murray J. Allen, Cpl. Norman B. Jones, PFC George B. Phillips, Cpl. James E. McCrae, Cpl. William Montgomery, PFCs Clifford H. Moorhead, Roy H. Wilson and Thomas M. Miller; middle row, PFCs James L. Price, Walter A. Benjamin, Leroy Green, Cpls. Fred N. Lowe, David Mann, PFC Samuel Y. Burnett, Tech. 5th James E. Scott, Cpl. Robert M. Lawrence, Jr., and Sgt. Richard S. Monclova; bottom row, Sgt. Joseph N. Thompson, Cpl. Andrean W. Cottrell, PFCs John W. Jones, Duane L. Roberts, Theotis T. Wilson, Joseph E. Buckins, Julius N. Prator, Arthur L. Bouldin, Tech. 5th Kenneth L. Janey and Staff Sgt. James D. Dunlap (the section leader). Shown in the bottom photo are students who specialized in Camera Repair. They are, left to right, top row, Cpl. Garrett H. Fennell, Sgt. Roy A. Robinson, PFCs William F. Raynor, Victor A. O'Brien and Roy W. Miller; middle row, PFC Raymond R. Steward, Cpl. O'Neal Barnes, Staff Sgt. Leroy E. Baker, PFC Eddie J. Fulton and Cpl. Corsey R. Coy; bottom row, PFCs John L. Slappey, William L. Kidd, Sgt. Theodore R. Penick and PFC Russell A. Green.

16 APRIL, 1943

Lowry Praised For Assistance To Bomber Unit

Lowry Field has received high praise for its cooperation with the heavy bombardment unit which recently completed a phase of its tactical training here.

The cooperation and assistance given at Lowry was better than the unit had received at any other station during its training, according to a memorandum from Maj. Gen. George E. Stratemeyer, Chief of the Air Staff at Army Air Forces headquarters in Washington, who recently inspected the bombardment group.

Brig. Gen. Harvey S. Burwell, Lowry's commanding general, reported to General Stratemeyer that having the bomber group on the field is a definite advantage to Lowry in that it permits technical training students going through school to see tactical equipment in use, and recommended the continuance of tactical training at Lowry.

Addition to Chapter 3

The Lowry Railroad

1918 – The first train to Govt. Hosp. #21 (Fitzsimons AMC) built by army engineers, was a spur off the Union Pacific R. R. (Kansas Branch) called the Sable Siding, north of the hospital. The hospital was dedicated in the fall of 1918. Bldg. 500 was built in 1940 and is still standing.

1920 - July - the hosp. was renamed in honor of Lt. William T. Fitzsimons, 1st medical officer killed in WW I, on 4Sep.,1917, in a German air raid.

1938 - Right of way bought for Lowry RR

1940 - Construction of RR began by WPA. First train arrived late in1940.
  Lowry branch began inside north boundary of Fitz, went east, then south to 6th and Potomac turned, west, ran on the north side of 6th to Lowry, split, north to coal trestle, south to warehouse. Cost, $269,000 and $45,000 for engine house. Buckley spur branched off at 6th & Potomac, crossed to south side of 6th at what is now I-225 and east to Buckley. Coal was the main cargo.

 1940 - Bldg. 500, Fitz. large hospital. Was then the largest bldg. in Colo.
.

 1942 - Jul.,1st steam engine. Passenger coaches added later. Lowry was the only base where a RR crossed the runways.

> Activity - Pre-WW II, 4 cars a week
> Wartime - 100 cars/day
> 1954 - 175/month
> End of '50s - 100/month

1964, 25Sep. RR ceased operation. Road bed on 6th is now a bike path.
> Ref. Intermountain News 11/12/1985, Intermountain.
> Chapter, National Railway Historical Society.
> (Bond Photos - BB-284A, BB-284B)

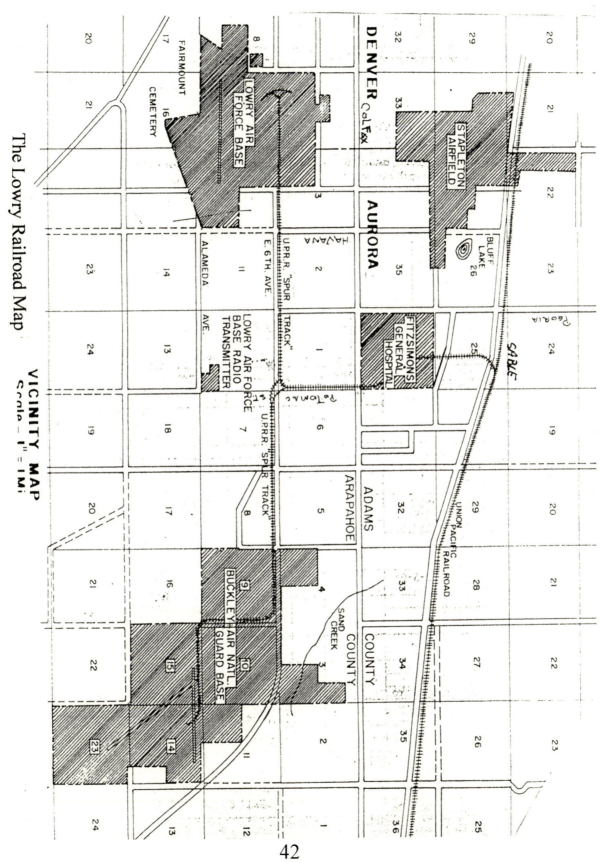

The Lowry Railroad Map

VICINITY MAP
Scale — 1" = 1 Mi

Chapter 4

1951 to 1960

1951

John Bond's house was built in 1951 at 191 Newport, the 10th house from First Avenue. John, his wife Grace, and their children moved in in 1964, shortly after his retirement from the Air Force in '63. The addition in the back was added from 1975-1980. John and Grace still live there today. Building # 407 was built on First Avenue and Quebec for the 7625th Ops. Squadron.

Also in 1951, Wherry Housing was built on the east side of Quebec from 6th Ave. to just north of 8th Ave. (Bldg.#1501 – 1585) for families. Part of the 1500 series remains in use today as low income housing called Blue Spruce Townhomes.

Jul. 31 – The Air Force Center on York Street opened

Dec. 3 – A B-29 returning from a training mission crashed in a residential neighborhood. The plane was coming from the west over the city when its engines began to fail. Aiming for Lowry's east-west runway, it crashed in Hilltop on First Avenue; plowing from Dahlia to Elm Street and barely missing a school. Of the 14 crew members, 8 were killed and 6 were injured. Five houses were partially or completely destroyed. Only 1 civilian and a fireman were injured. Fortunately, there were no bombs on board. Considerable discussion followed concerning how appropriate it was to have an air force base situated so close to a growing residential neighborhood. (Colorado Heritage Magazine/Summer 2006)

1952

An F-84 was placed on a pedestal in front of HQ. Bombs had already replaced the cannons in the same area.

1953

Bldg. # 1111, 1112, 1113, and 1119 were built for B.O.Q and family housing on the west side of Quebec St. Also Service Station #2 was opened on Yosemite St.

Jul.12 – The Glenn Miller Story, starring Jimmy Stewart and June Allison began filming. 1500 airmen were used as extras in parades and interior (#401) scenes. Other filming was done at Kittredge Castle in Montclair. In 1953, The Black Hangar (Bldg. 1499) was built and used for nuclear training. The hangar was converted to the Little Bear Skating Rink when the base closed.

Oct.23 – Walter B. Lowry (father of Francis) died.

Operation White House
President Eisenhower's Summer W. H.
8/1953 to 11/1955

Jun1, The date of the first notification that Lowry was to be the summer White House for President Eisenhower. Building 259 (Sanatorium/HQ), room 230 in the northwest corner was chosen as the location.

Aug8 – The President arrived in a C-121A (round windows) at 1600 hours and was greeted by Gov. Dan Thornton and Col. K. A. Cavenah. It was raining in sunny Colorado. The president spent most of his leisure time while here at his in-laws, the Douds, at 750 Lafayette St. in Denver. He went to religious services at the Doud's church, appearing rarely (some say once) at the chapel at Lowry to be later named in his honor. In 1955, when he had his heart attack it began at the Doud's residence.

Sep19 – The president departs for Washington D. C.

Aug21, 1954 – The second arrival. The president arrives in a C-121A (round windows) on a sunny day. In '53and'54, plane was Columbine II

Sep12 – The National Security Council met at 1600 hrs. in the Williamsburg Room at the Officers Club. This was the 1st time outside of Washington D. C. During the meeting, the president received a report from J. F. Dulles on his trip to Formosa to meet with Chan-Kai-Shek. The Williamsburg Room was later changed to the Eisenhower Room.

Oct15 – The president departed.

Aug14, 1955 – The president's third arrival in a C-121E, Columbine III

Sep23 – President Eisenhower suffered a heart attack and was admitted to Fitzsimons Army Hospital in Aurora, Colorado.

Nov11 – The President departed. (from hospital)

Mamie Doud Eisenhower

Mamie Geneva Doud was born in Boone, Iowa on Nov.14, 1896.The Doud family moved to Denver in 1902. They lived at 750 Lafayette St. She met Dwight D. Eisenhower on Oct. 3, 1915 at Fort Sam Houston, Texas. They were engaged on Feb. 14, 1916 and married at the Doud home on Jul. 1

Major and Mrs. Eisenhower were stationed at Fort Logan in 1920. The major was a recruiting officer. Mamie Eisenhower and her son, Lt. John Eisenhower visited Lowry briefly on Oct., 1944 (see, Rev-Meter). Mamie died on Nov.1, 1979.

1954

The Whiteman School was built at 4th Ave. and Newport St. and dedicated in 1955. The school was named in honor of Wilberforce Whiteman, music director of Denver Public Schools and father of Paul Whiteman, noted musician and composer.

Apr.1 – The official birthday of the United Stated Air Force Academy. The academy was created by Public Law 325 of the 83rd Congress. Lt. Gen. Hubert Harmon, AF adviser to Harold E. Talbot, Sec of the Air Force was appointed the 1st superintendent. (1955-1956).

Sep. – Intelligence trailers and transportation training was moved to Sheppard AFB to make room for the academy.

1955

USAFA at Lowry AFB

May 25th, 1949, the Service Academy Board (Stearns Board) recommended that an air force academy be established without delay. The selection for the site began in 1950 with the creation of a board chaired by Gen. Carl A. Spaats. It initially reviewed 350 proposed sites narrowing the choice to 29 then to 7. Again in 1954, the Sec. of the Air Force established a final committee that narrowed the choice to Alton, Ill., Geneva, Wisc. and Colorado Springs. On June 22nd, Secretary Talbot announced the site selection north of Colorado Springs and Lowry AFB as the interim site.

The Air Force Academy dedication at Lowry was a three day event. It began on Saturday July 9th, 1955 when the public was invited to inspect buildings, exhibits, briefings, and listen to music provided by service bands. On Sunday, July 10th, dignitaries and invited guests inspected the interim site and models of the AFA in Colorado Springs.

July 11th, Monday the academy was officially dedicated. Swearing in of the cadets began at 0700 hours in Bldg. 901. Valmore W. Borque was the first cadet to be sworn in (Borque from South Hadley, Mass. was also the 1st academy casualty of war). The cadets then donned one-piece powder blue coveralls and were drilled for the day's ceremonies.

Dedication was at 1600 hours for a class of 306 (305 plus Leo Prescott who missed due to measles) who marched in formation. During the ceremony, there was a flyover consisting of a B-36, a B-47, and the Thunderbirds.

Sept. 25th Classes began.

Bldg. 901, South Hall became the Science Building.

Bldg. 903, Polifka Hall was used for classrooms and a library.

Bldg. 905, Patrick Hall became administration.

A Red Matador missile was placed in the yard.

The Falcon was selected mascot for the academy.

In September, President Eisenhower viewed a cadet parade at Lowry.

On July, 1956, Major Gen. James E. Briggs replaced an ailing Gen. Harmon as superintendent.

Sept. 1956, Regulation, G.I. 2 piece fatigues replaced the powder blue coveralls (none of the coveralls have been saved for posterity). The cadet "Wings and Propeller" insignia was placed on service caps and suntan collars. The class of 1959 successfully completed it's 1st academic year.

Lt. Gen. Hubert Reilly Harmon

Gen. Harmon was born on Apr. 3, 1892 in Chester, Pa. He graduated from West Point in 1915 with Eisenhower and Bradley. He was known at the academy as "Doodles' Poodle". Of the 164 graduates of the class of 1915, 59 became general officers. Gen. Harmon's father, Millard F. Harmon, graduated from West Point in 1880. Gen. Harmon graduated from the Air Service Flying School at San Diego in 1917, was on Lt. Col.

William Mitchell's staff and was Pershing's air officer in 1917, in the AEF. In Dec. 1949, he was appointed Special Asst. to the Chief of Staff, USAF, for AFA matters. Gen. Harmon died on Feb. 22, 1957.

1957 – The blue winter Battle Jacket (Ike Jacket) became standard with "wing and Prop" insignia. The modified officer's cap insignia was adopted. The 1st cadets moved into the Squadron K area.

In 1958, the move to Colorado Springs began in August. On the 29th a small advanced party of 1st and 2nd class cadets moved to the new site. On the 30th, the class of '60 and '61 arrived back from summer leave. On the 31st, the 1st and the 4th classes arrived from field training directly to the Colorado Sprigs site known as the "Forward Airstrip Encampment". Cadet Hosmer recorded the move in the Talon (school paper), Oct., 1958 Edition). Hosmer was the first cadet to become an academy superintendent.

On May 19, 1959, President Eisenhower, unable to attend graduation, addressed cadets in Mitchell Hall at Colorado Springs.

On June 3, 1959, the AF Academy graduated the first 207 cadets.

End of AFA at Lowry

1956

Nov.15 – An RB-36 taking off from Lowry enroute to Ellsworth AFB, South Dakota crashes and burns. Shortly after takeoff, the engines quit due to fuel starvation that was probably caused from frozen fuel lines. The pilot, Capt. Regis Powers, attempted to make a crash-landing at Stapleton Airport. Failing the attempt, he brought the huge aircraft down in the field at the Rocky Mountain Arsenal, where it caught fire. There were 21 occupants. No fatalities, 2 serious injuries admitted to Fitzsimmons Army

Hosp. and many slightly injured. There were no ground fatalities. (Denver Post Nov.15, 16, 1956)

1957

Feb.11 – The NCO Club, Bldg.600, caught fire.

May18 – 3 AFA F-86(Sabre Jets) flew for Air Force Day.

1958

In the latter half of 1958, the rebuilt NCO club opened.
Sep.25 – The 703rd Strategic Missile Wing, S.A.C., was activated and construction of the Titan Missile Site at the Lowry Bombing Range began.

1959

Jan.1 – Lowry AFB became L.T.T.C. (Lowry Tech. Training Center).

Jan.24 – The B-25 formally used for training was replaced by the T-33.

Apr.3 – The north-south runway was ordered closed.

Jun.30 – The Naval Air Station-Denver (NAS-D) at Buckley was deactivated. The base reverted to the Air Force and was licensed to the state of Colorado.

1960

Sometime after Dec. 1959, a second floor was added to the front of Bldg. 402 (hangar).

Apr.18 – Buckley Field became a Colorado Air National Guard base.

June 1 – Lowry AFB was closed to jet transient traffic. Flights were diverted to Buckley ANG Base for servicing. (Denver Post, May 16, 1960.)

DEDICATED TO PEACE   16 THE

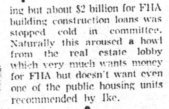

AIR FORCE ★ ACADEMY

'T

He's

N OTHIN
beings
some
tention recer

A young
honor to be
three ordina
trip. The airp
down a red c

The air
bound for th
off, it flew f

Glimpsi
not at all fr
for someon
charge. Turnin
panion, she ord
"Call   the
s t e wardess,
and have her
tell the pilot
he's flying
the wrong
way."

I HEARD
also of a
lady who, to
put it mildly,
has a figure
like a lath.
She and her
consort were
on the way
rus - growing
other, and the
on, both ways.
is confiscated
the first (or
contaminated
the state of the
part.

This coupl
anges. The
would save tw
adjusted ther
dice in stra
saved her o
was a minor
pared to the
maybe baffle
from males t
a new experi

DREW PEARSON
Dems Help Ike on Housing

WASHINGTON.—The back-stage jockeying between the White House and Capitol Hill over public housing is one of the most interesting develop-ments of this congressional session.

As usual it finds the

ing but about $2 billion for FHA building construction loans was stopped cold in committee. Naturally this aroused a howl from the real estate lobby which very much wants money for FHA but doesn't want even one of the public housing units recommended by Ike.

●

AMONG the GOP congress-

It was just before this dead-lock occurred that alert John McCormack, who knows in ad-vance how crucial votes are go-ing to stack up, phoned the White House and tried to warn Sherman Adams what was hap-pening.

However, he could not get Adams on the phone. Later Mc-Cormack called back, but still

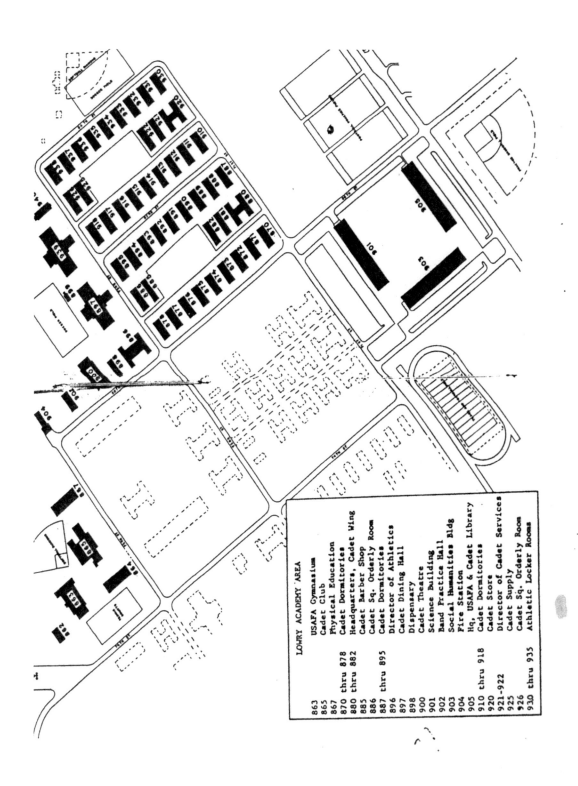

US Air Force Academy area at Lowry

Chapter 5

1961 to 1970

1961

The Cold War and the advances in technology added new challenges to the Lowry programs.

The Air Force Ballistic Committee was formed in 1955. On March 13th 1958, it selected the Lowry Bombing Range to be the first Titan I (ICBM) launch complex, and the first Titan I missile wing. The 703rd Strategic Missile Wing was designated the 451st SMW on July 1, 1961.

The 451st was originally activated on May 1, 1943 as a bomber group (heavy)of B-24s. It served in W.W.II, raiding northern Italy and eastern Europe including the Ploesti raids.

The 848th SMS and the 849th SMS were redesignated the 724th SMS and the725[th] SMS. On Aug. 4, 1961, construction of all 9 silos at the three launch complexes for the 724th east and southeast of Denver were completed. On April 18, 1962, SAC declared the 724th SMS operational and 2 days later it went on alert. (9 missiles) In May, the 725th SMS went on alert. (a SAC first) (703/451 SMW Op. Hist., USAFHRA9/58-6/65)

By 1962, Lowry's Dept. of Missile Training was graduating 1,000 airmen/year.

In 1961, Lowry Headquarters began to move to Bldg. 349. The former barracks was partitioned for HQ. L.T.T.C.

From 1961 to 1964 the O' Club was rebuilt and a stag bar was added.

1962

May4 – East-West runway was resurfaced.

Oct.27 - On land occupied by the Windsor Milk Farm in 1893, south of Lowry, Windsor Gardens was dedicated. Moving in, in Dec.

1963

Apr.11 to Jun.10 – The buildings that served as The Agnes Memorial Sanatorium and the Lowry HQ was demolished. (1903-1963) Building 250, that served as the medical director's residence, Hotel De Gink, and the commanding officer's home, was spared and remains as a private home today. (2016)

Jul.1 – The Armed Forces Air Intelligence Training Center was established at Lowry.

Oct.23 – Lowry's Intelligence School conducted first joint classes for Air Force and Navy students.

1964

Sep.25 – The Lowry (Lowry-Buckley-Fitzsimmons) Railroad ceased operation. See Addition to Chapter 3.

Oct.24 – Valmore W. Borque, AFA Class of '60 was killed in Viet Nam, the first combat casualty of an academy graduate.

Nov.19 – Sec. McNamara announced the faze out of first generation SM-65 Atlas and SM-68Titan I, missiles by June, 1965. On Nov. 12, D.O.D announced the end of flying activity at Lowry by June,1960. It was based on "operational requirements, flying safety interests, and economic considerations". Flying activity was moved to Buckley, (COANG). (Lowry Airman, Nov. 27, 1964)

The Bond Family moved to 191 Newport St. (See Chapter 11)

The sign "Bring Me Men" was erected at the Air Force Academy.

1965

Feb. – In accordance with the phase out of flying, the first T-33s were transferred to Peterson Field, Colorado Springs.

March 26 – The last formation fly over by T-33 aircraft took place.

Apr.14 – SAC removed the missiles from all 18 silos.

Jun.25 – The 724th SMS and the 725th SMS were deactivated.

Sep.1 – The Air Reserve Records Center became the Air Reserve Personnel Center.

1966

Flying facilities were officially closed at Lowry.

May – The Colorado Aviation Historical Society was established

May10 – The last H-21C helicopter left for Davis-Monthan. A H-21C from Lowry #534357 is now at the Pueblo Weisbrod Aviation Museum.

Jun.30 – Major General Charles H. Anderson flew the last plane, a T-29, to the Buckley Air National Guard Base.

Sometime in 1966, after flying ceased, hangar numbers changed. Hangar #1, Bldg. 402, became Hangar #2. Hangar #2, Bldg. 401 became Hangar #1. The new numbers remain so today.

1967

May8 – Museum of Aerospace Photography at Lowry was approved by the Secretary of the Air Force. "Its mission will be to collect, preserve and exhibit material of historical significance."

May25 – Kelly Rd. and the Alameda areas were declared surplus.

Jun. – The beacon which flashed red, green and white was removed and sold to a local wrecking company.

Jul.1 – The Air Force transferred the 3320th Retraining Group for convict airmen from Amarillo AFB to Lowry. Also transferred was supply training,

1968

Aug.1 – The Air Reserve Personnel Center became separate, reporting directly to the Chief of Air Force Reserve.

1970

Sep.4 – The first (of five) one- thousand- man dorm., Bldg. 400, was completed and dedicated to Airman 1st Class Larry Cox

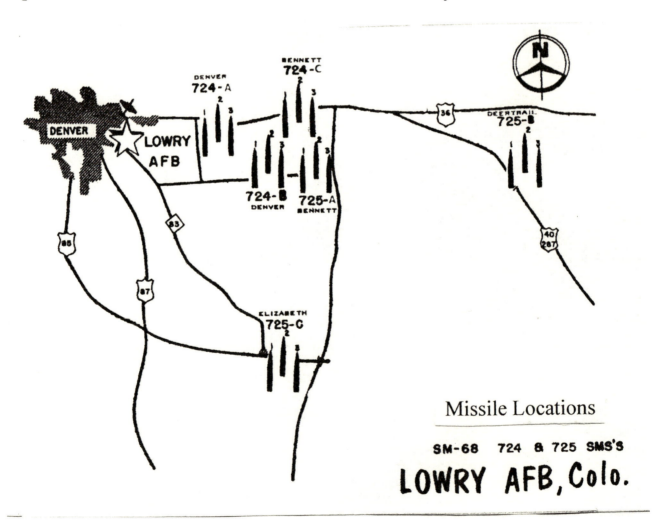

Missile Locations

SM-68 724 & 725 SMS'S
LOWRY AFB, Colo.

LOWRY AFB

TITAN I

451st STRATEGIC MISSILE WING

DENVER, COLORADO

848TH* AND 849TH* STRATEGIC MISSILE SQUADRONS.

THE **848TH** WAS IN OPERATION FROM **FEBRUARY 1960 TO JULY 1961**.
THE **849TH** WAS IN OPERATION FROM **AUGUST 1960 TO JULY 1961**.

THE **724TH** WAS IN OPERATION FROM **JULY 1961 TO JUNE 1965**. THE
725TH WAS IN OPERATION FROM **JULY 1961 TO JUNE 1965**.

*THE **848TH SMS** AND THE **849TH SMS** BECAME THE **724TH SMS** AND THE **725TH SMS** IN JULY 1961 RESPECTFULLY.

BASE	MODEL	LAUNCHER DESIGNATION	SITE NUMBER	LOCATION
Lowry AFB,	I	724-A-1,2,3	1	Bennett
Colorado	I	724-B-1,2,3	2	Denver
	I	724-C-1,2,3	3	Denver
	I	725-A-1,2,3	4	Deertail
	I	725-B-1,2,3	5	Bennett

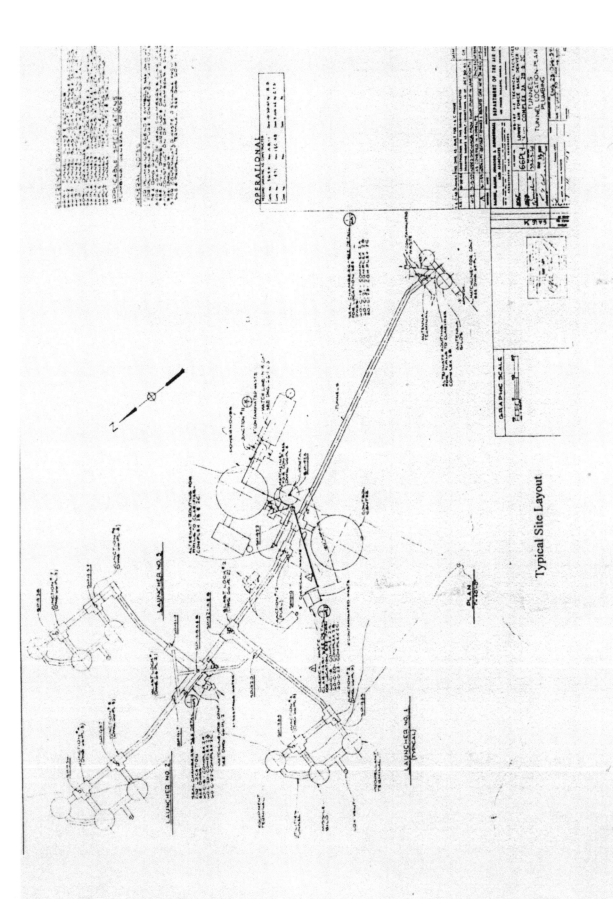

Typical Site Layout

Chapter 6

1971 to 1980

1971

Apr.1 – The Air Force activated the 3415th Special Training Group.

Jul. – The Lowry Hospital was closed and the building declared surplus. Squadron K, Supply Room (where John Bond met Grace Cook), Bldg.920, was destroyed.

Aug.20 – Chaplin Thomas first proposed that Chapel 1 be given preservation status. (see Chapter 6)

Nov.20 – Warehouse, Bldg. 594 was destroyed by fire.

1972

Aug.1 – 3415th Technical Training School became the Air Force School of Aerospace Sciences.

Oct. – Mess Hall #2, Bldg. #477 changed to #577

1973

Feb. – 3415th Special Training Group began drug rehabilitation as part of their training.

Mar.28 – The School of Applied Aerospace Sciences gained accreditation from the North Central Association of Colleges and Schools.

May21,1972 – Construction started on the Center Chapel, Bldg. 697. It was dedicated in May, 19^{th,}1973 (see chapter 8.) Also in 1973, Lowry Air Force Base officially became The Lowry Technical Training Center.

1974

Many older buildings were destroyed in 1974. With the exception of Bldg. 880, then the Lowry Heritage Museum, all of the academy barracks were destroyed. One barrack was bought and moved to Glendale to became a sports bar on E. Virginia Ave. Service Station 1 and 2 were removed.

1975

Feb.1 – The 3415th Special Training Group merged with the 3320th Retraining Group.

1976

Jun.15 – The 3320 Retraining Group became the 3320th Correction and Rehabilitation Group.

Sep.1 – The Air Force Reserve Personnel Center and the Air Force Accounting and Finance Center moved into the Gilchrist Building (Bldg.444), west of Quebec St. and south of 1st Ave. The building was dedicated on the 30th of the same month.

1977

Mar.1 – The 3320th Correction and Rehab. Group was reduced to squadron level.

Apr.1 – 3400th Technical Training Wing was activated. (Picture in Rev-Meter)

.1978

Feb. – A F-15 arrived for ground training of munitions loading classes. Also in February, the 3320th Correction and Rehab. Squadron closed its confinement center.

May 14-21 – Air Force Week, Open House on 20-21.

Sep.1-Eight- hour classroom day replaced the 6 hour academic day in effect since W.W. II.

1979

Mar. – The Air Force recommended keeping Lowry open, ending months of speculation about closure. (Levy and Scanlan, "Pursuit of Excellence." A History of Lowry AFB, 1937-1987)

1980

Jan. – Lowry acquired a B-52D for weapons loading and release training.

May 11-17 – Air Force Week.

The Gilchrist Building (#444)

Chapter 7

1981 to 1994 and Beyond

1981

Mar.11-13 – The control towers on Hangar 402 and 401 were removed. There had been no air traffic for 18 years and leaking was a problem. (Lowry Airman, March 13, 1981) The numbers on Hangar 1 and 2 had been changed sometime after 1966 and before 1968. The Lowry Airman, April, 1968 shows Hangar 401 with the # 1 on it. This we know; the hangar to the southwest of the two was built from Aug. 1938 to Aug. 1939, the first new hangar at Lowry. It was equipped with a small control tower in the center of the roof. The official number was 402 and being first it was labeled #1. Hangar 401 to the ENE of 402 was built from Jun. 1940 to Apr. 1941 and was named #2, with a tall control tower on the southeast corner. After the base closed, the official numbers began to fade and are now only known as Hangar #1(Wings Museum) and Hangar #2(storage and retail). In 1985, a classroom extension was added on to 401 and completed in 1986.

1982

May6 – Chapcl #1 was placed on the register of historic places.

Aug. – Lowry received two F-16 aircraft as ground trainers.

Sep.12 – Eisenhower Chapel was dedicated. (See Chapter 8)

Sep.13 – Lowry Heritage Museum (LHM) was opened in Bldg.880. The first aircraft was obtained in 1984. (See Chapter 10)

1984

Jun.22 – *A*ir Force Academy reunion of class of '59. An academy room in Bldg.880 was dedicated. This room was the Commandant of cadet's office during academy days. LHM held an open house.

Jun.24 – Steve Draper(GS-9) was hired as the curator of LHM.

Dec.26 – Lowry officials opened the new Armed Forces Air Intelligence Center Facility, (Bldg.408) the Ballard Space Center.

1985

Feb.9 – Construction work on the Commissary, Post Exchange and NCO Club expansion was completed. Officers club reopened on May 22nd.

July – Expansion on Hangar 401 started.

1986

Oct.9 – First class of 25 officers began Undergraduate Space Training at Lowry.
Dec. –T SQ 54 was delivered.

1987

Feb.20 – The first Undergraduate Space Training class graduated at Lowry.

Oct.2 – After many hours of volunteer effort in the reconstruction, T SQ 54 was dedicated (See Chapter 10). Also at that time, Lowry celebrated its 50th Anniversary. The first Tattoo ceremony was performed.

1989

Nov.30 – Keith Ferris – 5th Annual Art show at the Officer's Club.

1991

Apr.12 – Defense Secretary Cheney placed Lowry on the closure list.

Jul.15 – The list (with Lowry on it) sent to congress with 45 days to approve or change.

Aug.3 – Reunion of the academy class of '61. Col. Neel presented a plaque to the museum.

1992

Jun. – Lt. Col. George Peck became the new Public Information officer. He was also placed in charge of LHM.

1993

Jul.30 – Jeff Hunt was made curator of the museum. (Article with photo in the Lowry Airman.)

1994

Jun.28 – The Lowry School and Training Command organizations were deactivated.

Sep.30 – **Lowry Air Force Base was closed.**

1995

Feb. – Stapleton International Airport was closed.

Mar. – Denver International Airport opened.

1999

Fitzsimons Army Hospital campus was closed except for the Army Reserve Center, which was moved to the southeast of the property. The land now serves as the home of the University of Colorado Medical Complex, The Children's Hospital and the future Veterans Hospital.

2003

Mar.28 – The sign "Bring Me Men" was removed at the Air Force Academy.

Unique squadron offers se

By Sgt. Sue Miller

More than 15,000 court-martialed airmen have been given an opportunity to continue their military career under a program being conducted here by the 3320th Correction and Rehabilitation Squadron.

This "second chance" offer is a unique rehabilitation program for Air Force members who have been convicted by court-martial under the Uniform Code of Military Justice.

The voluntary program is the basic way back to active duty, according to Maj. Jim J. Caton, 3320th CRS commander. "It's a second chance program for selected airmen who are recommended by their commanders and have a desire to return to a productive Air Force life."

The 3320th CRS is the only organization of its kind in the Air Force. It was established at Amarillo AFB, Texas in February 1952 and moved to Lowry in 1967.

"We receive personnel from all over the world and our job is to prepare these airmen for return to duty improved in attitude, behavior and productivity," said Maj. Walter Scott, chief of the rehabilitation branch.

When a member arrives at the squadron, he or she undergoes a series of psychological and academic tests. From the results, an individualized treatment program is devised.

In the next four to five months the individual will attend seminars, group sessions, individual counseling sessions, workshops, gym and eventually be assigned a job on the base.

The squadron's program is designed to help the rehabilitee help himself and to provide the kind of treatment that will return him to duty.

Every week the progress of each rehabilitee is evaluated on pertinent aspects of the program. Rehabilitees are personally responsible for their progress.

The program operates on a privilege-level system that is designed to reinforce the rehabilitee's active participation by rewarding positive changes in behavior and progress toward the goals identified in the therapeutic plan.

There are three criteria for determining whether a rehabilitee will be recommended for continued duty, according to Major Scott. First, each staff member asks: "Would I want this airman working for me?" Secondly, "Has this airman resolved the attitudinal and behavioral problems that got him court-martialed in the first place?"

And thirdly, "Can this airman be returned to duty as a productive airman without further difficulty in any area?" If the answers are "yes," the airman is recommended for return to duty.

Rehabilitees not recommended for return to duty must accept the original discharge adjudged by the convening authority.

Successful completion of the rehabilitation program will permit an individual to return to duty, and with continuing satisfactory service, to receive an honorable discharge upon the completion of his enlistment.

"Approximately 50 percent of the individuals that go through this program are returned to duty. And of those, more than 80 percent successfully complete their tour of duty," said Major Scott.

Progress check

Maj. Walter Scott, chief Donald Fleck, conduct a we

SrA. Ed Parrales, right, m discuss material covered ir

Reserve procedures

3320th Correction and Rehabilitation Squadron

Chapter 8

Religious Buildings at Lowry

Bldg.27 - Chapel #1 – Eisenhower Chapel (Protestant). Started construction July 8, 1941. Dedicated 1000 hrs., Nov. 23,1941. Lt. Horace N. Cooper, Clark O. Hitt.(chaplains). Pvt. Joe German sang.

Bldg.481 - Chapel #2 – (Catholic) dedicated 0900 hrs., Nov. 23, 1941. Chaplin Christian A. Wachter celebrated mass. Torn down April, 1974.

Bldg.498 – "Large Barnlike Structure"

Chaplin Wachter arrived at Lowry around May 1941, conducted mass first in a tent near 6th and Quebec. Then it was "Old Hangar", Bldg. 366 until July 1941 when services were moved to Bldg. 498 until Nov.Then Chapel #2 was dedicated. (Rev-meter, 29May,1942).
"Old Hangar" could be Bldg. 366 which was the first hangar built on Lowry from the old field.
The location of Bldg. 498 is unknown. It could be a previous number for Bldg. 365 which was converted from a hangar to a gym. Bldg. 498 is listed on a 1943 map as a Rec. Center and theatre. Number is unclear. The 49__ series was located in the vicinity of Rosemary and Renegade Way, N.W. of chapel #2.

Bldg.755 - Chapel #3 – Built July 1942
Destroyed Nov. 1, 1974

Bldg.940 - Chapel #4 – Built July 1942
Destroyed Nov. 1974.
Bldg.940 – Was the Cadet Chapel from 1955 to 1958.
Bldg.697 – Center Chapel, grounding 5/21/72, dedicated 5/1973, replaced chapels #2,3 and 4. This chapel is in use today. (Lowry Airman, 6/1/73)
1943,6Aug. "Madonna for the Soldier" presented for chapel #940
1971,20Aug. Chaplin Thomas first proposed preservation status for Chapel #1.
1982,6May Chapel #1 placed on register of Historic Places.
1982,12Sep. Eisenhower Chapel dedicated.

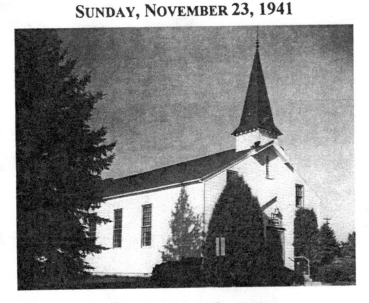

Dedication of the Chapels
Buildings No. 27 and No. 481

LOWRY FIELD, Denver, Colorado
Sunday, November 23, 1941

Commanding Officer
Colonel Early E. W. Duncan, A.C.

Chaplains

Major Christian A. Wachter, C. of Ch.
Lieutenant Horace N. Cooper, C. of Ch.
Lieutenant Clark O. Hitt, C. of Ch.

Chapter 9

Buckley Air Force Base

1937

Aug.26 – Congress authorized $2,275,000 for construction of Lowry plus a tract of land for an Aerial Gunnery and Bombing range.

1938

59,814,430 acres is donated to the war department for the "Lowry Bombing Range".

1941

Early in the year, the City and County of Denver purchases 5,740 acres east of the city and donates it to the war department for use as an auxiliary landing field, briefly called Lowry Aux. Field. [1]

1942

Due to the demands of the war, the decision was made to fund the construction at the auxiliary field. $7.5 million was appropriated.

Apr. – The contract for construction was signed and building began in May. When it was finished in July, it had 700 buildings, a railroad spur, (See Lowry R.R., Addition to Chapter 3) coal fired steam heating plant, streets, runways, etc.

Jul.1 – The base was activated. General Order No.1 designated Col. (later Brig. Gen.) L.A. Lawson commanding officer. Classes began on July 7th. The name was changed to Buckley Field in honor of 1st Lt. John H. Buckley.

John H. "Buck" Buckley was born in Longmont, Colorado, July 8th, 1895. He was a student at the University of Colorado when war began in April, 1917. He enlisted that month and after training, he was sent to France and assigned to the 28th Aero Squadron. He was promoted to 1st Lt. in July, 1918. Lt. Buckley lost his life on September 17, 1918, during the Argonne Offensive. When flying in formation, he collided with a friendly aircraft. [1] Buckley's grandfather, John A. Buckley was the founder of Longmont, Co.

.1943

During the war Buckley Field expanded to 3 sites for training at the Bombing Range and cold weather training first at Jones Pass in the Rocky Mountains and later moved to Echo Lake. Armament training was divided between Lowry and Buckley, bomber training at Lowry and fighter training at Buckley. At one point, Buckley had the largest fighter aircraft armament school in the country.

May.19 – the 460th Bombardment Group was established.

Jul.1 – The 460th was activated. It was inactivated in Sept., 1945

1946

Jul.1 – Buckley Field, placed on inactive status at war's end, again became an auxiliary field for Lowry.

Dec. - The newly formed Colorado Air National Guard(COANG) was granted a right-of-entry permit and assumed responsibility for the site.

1 – US Air Force Fact Sheet: Buckley A. F. B. Heritage

1947

The Dept. of the Navy took control and renamed the base Naval Air Station-Denver(NAS-D).

To relieve the area housing shortage for service men returning to civilian life, many buildings on base were remodeled. 5 villages for veterans were established with a mayor, a council for each village and a newspaper. The villages were Bucktel, Pioneer, North Denver, Fort Logan and Buckley Field. The program was ended in 1951.

1960

Apr.18 – The Navy left, and the base was transferred to the state of Colorado for use by the Air National Guard. Renamed Buckley Field. It was the first "stand alone" guard base in the Air Force. The 140th Tactical Fighter Wing(TFW) was the host unit.

1970

Building the geodesic domes in stages began.

1989

Publication of "Colorado Pride" a history of The CO. Air. Nat. Guard.

2000

Oct.1 – The Air Force resumed command and the base became the Buckley Air Force Base. 821SG was the host unit.

2001

Oct.1 – Activated 460th Air Base Wing (ABW) as host unit.

2004

Aug.19 – Command changed to the 460th Space Wing (SW).

Chapter 10

The Museum

1967

May.8 - Establishment of the Goddard Aerospace Photography Museum, approved at Lowry by the Secretary of the AF ("50 years of Photo Trn.")

May.25 – The museum was in a classroom of bldg. 349, Photo. Dept. HQ. or possibly in the basement of the photo school. S/SGT. Mike Cleveland (photo. instr.) was appointed curator as a collateral duty. (Lowry Airman 25 May'67). It soon closed.

Origen of the Lowry Heritage Museum (L.H.M.)

The exact date of the start of both Project Warrior and L.H.M. is in question. Project Warrior, a voluntary A.F. program, was initiated by General Lew Allen Jr. before he retired (1Jul82) to improve the morale and efficiency of the service. AF records state that Nov.,82 was the start. This appears to be inaccurate. Spring, 1982 or earlier would be the best guess. (AF Magazine, Vol.65#8, 8/1982.)

The best date for the start of the L.H.M. is **June,1982**. At that time a meeting was held, chaired by Col. Hobgood, and attended by senior staff, representatives from Project Warrior, T/SGT Cleveland, Base Historian, Col. John W. Douglas and probably Russ Tarvin and Capt. Hitt. At that meeting, it was decided that 1. Lowry should have a museum built around the 1967 camera collection, 2. A museum foundation should be established, 3. T/SGT Cleveland to be the curator 4. Museum to be housed in Bldg. 880, south wing and 5. to aim for an opening date of 13 Sep, 1982. There is a note about a meeting held in Nov.,1981 chaired by Col. C. W. Reed attended by Col. Hobgood, Base Historian Roger Miller and others to discuss a museum. The notes state that "no decisions were made".

1982

Aug.18 – The name "Wings over the Rockies" mentioned in Lowry Airman and again in 17 Nov. 83.

Sep.13 – The Lowry Heritage Museum opened, on the 35th Anniversary

of Air F. T/Sgt. Cleveland was the director.
Sep.18 - Lowry Heritage Committee built the 1st exhibit around a camera collection (wing of bldg. 880, located near Dayton St. and 9th Ave.).
Sep.23 - LHM Foundation incorporated. Volunteers added (Russ Tarvin Col. Ret. and Capt. Dwight Hitt)

1983

From Sept, 1982 to Sept.1983 the Museum had poor attendance, opened very little, etc. T/SGT Cleveland was assigned other duties on base.

Sep. - Steve Draper(GS-9) arrived, worked for free until 1/84 then was given $50/mo. Draper was a person with museum experience.

1984

In 1984, the Museum increased its hours, started educational
 programs and had exhibits such as LAFB history, a uniform exhibit, a military vehicle display, etc. Attendance improved. The museum was placed under the command of the Deputy Base Commander's office and contact was made with the USAF Museum Program.
Jun.22 –The AFA Class of '59 reunion, dedicated a room (formally the Commandant of Cadets Office) in the LHM (Bldg. 880). The museum held an open house.

1987

The museum moved into the 2nd wing of building 880. (At the present it is the Morning Star senior day care center).

The T SQ 54 Story

The B-29, T SQ 54, arrived at the museum in Nov.-Dec.1986, by trucks, in parts from China Lakes, California where it was used for bombing practice. Prior to its location there, it had served 12 years (1945-1956), first on 37 bombing missions, plus supply missions in the Pacific during World War II, as part of the 73rd Bomb Wing, 498th Bomb Group. In 1949, it was converted to an aerial tanker. In 1956 it was phased out of service and became the responsibility of the U S Air Force Museum. Many volunteers (approx. 90) at L.H.M. stepped up and began a monumental restoration. A fund drive was initiated. When the work was done 11 months later, 15,000 volunteer hours under project director Mel Blancett had been contributed and $85,000 had been donated by local citizens, organizations and corporations. The restored (exterior) T SQ 54 was dedicated in a grand ceremony on Oct. 2, 1987

1988

May.14 – L.H.M. became part of USAF museum program.

1989

Apr. – John Bond joined the volunteer staff of the museum.

1992

Mar23. – Nose Art exhibit opens at L.H.M.

1993

Jun.10 – When plans were being made to close Lowry, the Air Force Museum (still the owner) made plans to move T SQ 54 to the Air Museum in Seattle which featured Boeing aircraft. L.H.M was to lose T SQ.54. A team arrives to disassemble and ship it to the Air Museum in Seattle. Understandably, sadness, frustration and anger ran through the museum and among the volunteers.

Jul.30 – Geoff Hunt became curator of the museum (article in the Lowry Airman).

Oct.15 – Lowry Lithographs by army M/Sgt. Sieger Hurtgers were offered for sale in the museum.

Nov.17 – Russ Tarvin suggested changing the name of the museum foundation from L.H.M. to Wings Over the Rockies (L.H.M Board minutes).

Dec.14 – Carl Williams (board member and major supporter) toured the museum with Russ Tarvin (Board minutes).

1994

The museum was renamed "Wings Over the Rockies"

Apr.20 – The move from Bldg.880 to Hangar #1 was started.

Jun.4 – Lowry Heritage Museum was closed.

Jul.8 – The Space Station was moved.

Oct. – The first edition of Wingspan was produced.

Dec.1 – Wings over the Rockies was officially opened.

The B-52 (#2005)

1965 - 67	In hangar for students.
1984,26 Oct.	On static display in middle of field.
1996	E. end of parking lot across from museum.
1998	Fire damage. Painted

2007
Mar. – The false ceiling was removed in the main hangar.
2010
Jun.25 – The eighty seat Harrison Fort Theatre was opened

Oct.19 – The B-52 was damaged in the first lift. Raised 2 days later, in front of the entrance.

2011

Apr.5 -   Remodeled WORM opening celebration.
Control Tower, new entrance, second floor, gallery,
 new floor covering,

Apr.25 – The contract for 1292 sq. ft. office space at Centennial Airport was signed for another expansion of the Wings organization.

2013
Apr.14 – Book signing for "Lowry Air Force Base" by authors Jack Ballard, John Bond and George Paxton.

Jun. – Aviation Extreme was installed in the former Lowry Room.

Oct.13 – Math-Midway began, and ran thru Dec. 31, sponsored by the Oppenheimer Funds.

2015

Aug.1 – Classes began for the Wings Aerospace Academy at the museum. It consisted of grades 6, 7and 8 with 45 students attending. Classes are once a week on air and space subjects. Students do their academic subjects at home on line. In the 2016-17 school year, attendance increased to 70 and grades 5 and 9 were added. The purpose of the academy is to prepare interested youngsters for a future in the expanding aerospace industry. Two areas are offered, flying and mech. engineering. The academy will extend to grade 12 in the future.

TALKING PAPER ON
LOWRY HERITAGE MUSEUM
14 October 1982

-The Lowry Heritage Museum Foundation is in the process of being chartered.

 --Capt Hitt, SJA/JAC, has more complete information.

-It looks like Building #880 will be our museum.

 --The CE letter is at HQ ATC and should be forwarded to the Air Staff momentarily.

 --Maj Cunningham called HQ ATC/PA (OPR in USAF for museums); they will support our letter.

 --Some problems remain with structure.

   ---TSgt Cleveland jury-rigged an alarm system out of old parts; it needs improvement.

   ---Heating system may not be satisfactory for winter.

-Resources are in a state of transition.

 --Many of the items on loan may have to be returned soon.

   ---SSgt Dyer who loaned insignia display leaves for AFA in December.

   ---Model planes may have to be returned to owners.

   ---Photos on loan from History Office can remain, but their absence reduces HO's flexibility.

 --We are receiving numerous offers of assistance.

   ---Peterson AFB sent a rotating display case.

   ---SSgt Shelton furnished info on five static display acft available.

   ---Eglin AFB armament museum closing, displays are available.

   ---Capt Yaskin coordinating displays to be built by Tech Training Groups.

   ---Problem is lack of anyone to coordinate securing these items.

-Basic problem in creating outstanding museum is lack of a full time staff.

 --TSgt Cleveland is back teaching full time.

 --Retiree Affairs Office not interested in moving to Building #880.

 --Museum, in short, is not open at this time.

75

-Actions required to have an outstanding museum.

--OPR must be assigned in accordance with AFR 210-4.

--A slot must be identified and moved under OPR as permanent curator slot.

--MSgt Sibitsky should be assigned to the museum TDY for 180 days to keep it functioning.

--TSgt Cleveland, now the additional duty curator, should be released out of his current assignment in the 3420 TCHTG Photo Sciences Branch and made full time museum curator within the next 180 days.

Everything that I have read or heard over the last few months says that we must have a full time curator in order to develop an outstanding museum.

--When #880 is saved, I will get with the Denver Landmark Commission to get the building recognized historically.

--As soon as the hard decisions are made, I will prepare the museum approval package for submission to HQ USAF Public Affairs.

ROGER G. MILLER, GS-11, DAF
LTTC Historian

Wings Museum in the late 90s, early 2000s

NEW WING OPENS

With the dedication of the Academy Room and the new entrance, the Museum has doubled its size.

The new entrance, now on the north side of the building, ~~houses~~ opens on a the Time Line history of Lowry from 1937 to the present. Lowry's story is told through photographs and artifacts.

The Academy Room depicts some of the history of the USAF Academy at Lowry. ~~The Exhibit~~ contains uniforms, and photographs of the cadets and staff during this important period ~~time~~ in Lowry's history.

Other new exhibits include the Armaments Room. The exhibit deals with munitions training through the years, it including an exhibit on the Norden Bombsight (see article by Karl Lawrence). There is also a new and improved photographic exhibits and uniform displays.

What is new inside is also new outside with the establishment of the museum's airpark. The first two aircraft, a F-4c and F-102, have been placed ~~put~~ on exhibit.

As one of the museum's volunteers put it "the difference from two months ago till now is remarkable." Come down and see for yourself. The Museums' hours are 9:00am-4:30pm Monday thru Friday, and 10:00am to 4:00pm on Saturday.

22 June 1989

77

GB-52B S/N 52-005
BUFF – "BIG UGLY FAT FELLOW"

- THIS AIRPLANE WAS DELIVERED TO THE USAF AS RB-52B ON MARCH 3, 1955 (R DESIGNATION FOR RECONNAISSANCE)
- SHE WAS CONVERTED TO A STANDARD B-52B AND SERVED AS AN AIRCREW FLIGHT TRAINER AT CASTLE AFB, CA UNTIL 1966 WHEN SHE WAS RETIRED
- ARRIVED AT LOWRY AFB ON APRIL 28, 1966 AND SERVED AS A GROUND INSTRUCTIONAL TRAINER, HENCE THE NEW DESIGNATION GB-52B
- IN DECEMBER OF 1994, THE AIRCRAFT BECAME PART OF WINGS OVER THE ROCKIES AIR AND SPACE MUSEUM
- SHE IS ONE OF ONLY FOUR B-52B AIRCRAFT LEFT (ALL ARE RB-52B)
- WINGSPAN: 185 FEET. THIS WINGSPAN IS LONGER THAN THE DISTANCE THAT WILBUR WRIGHT FLEW ON HIS HISTORIC FIRST FLIGHT AT KITTY HAWK, NC.
- HEIGHT: 48 FEET 3 INCHES
- WEIGHT: 272,000 LBS AND 420,000 LBS MAXIMUM
- POWERPLANT: 8 PRATT AND WHITNEY J57 TURBOJETS, RATED AT 11,400 LBS THRUST EACH
- SPEED: 630 MPH MAXIMUM
- COMBAT RADIUS: 3590 MILES WITH 10,000 LBS BOMB LOAD
- CREW: 6 MEMBERS INCLUDING PILOT, CO-PILOT, NAVIGATOR, BOMBARDIER, ELECTRONIC WEAPONS OFFICER, AND TAIL GUNNER
- WEAPONS: 4-.50 CALIBER M3 MACHINE GUNS IN THE TAIL TURRET, UP TO APPROXIMATELY 43,000 LBS OF ORDINANCE
- FOR MORE THAN 40 YEARS B-52 STRATOFORTRESSES HAVE BEEN THE BACKBONE OF THE MANNED STRATEGIC BOMBER FORCE FOR THE UNITED STATES
- THE B-52A FIRST FLEW IN 1954. A TOTAL OF 744 B-52S WERE BUILT WITH THE LAST, A B-52H, DELIVERED IN OCTOBER 1962.
- CURRENT ENGINEERING ANALYSES SHOW THE B-52'S LIFE SPAN TO EXTEND BEYOND THE YEAR 2040.
- ONLY THE H MODEL IS STILL IN THE ACTIVE USAF INVENTORY

B-29, T☐54, after restoration at Lowry Heritage Museum

B-52B (005), now in front of Wings Museum

79

B-29 Project Serves As A Painful Lesson To Restoration Volunteers

by Kevin P. Corbley

Aviation enthusiasts here learned a painful lesson this summer about the pitfalls of restoring aircraft for the military. More than 200 volunteer aircraft restoration workers found out the hard way that what the Air Force giveth, the Air Force can taketh away.

The Air Force decided to move a B-29 Superfortress away from Denver where it had been restored with more than $85,000 in private cash and 15,000 volunteer hours. The bomber was moved from the Lowry Heritage Museum at Lowry Air Force Base to the Museum of Flight in Seattle.

Volunteers who worked on the project were stunned to discover the Air Force could move the bomber that they believed they were entitled to keep, although the Air Force was the legal owner. The situation in Denver has sent a ripple effect through the aircraft restoration industry around the country and served notice to those who volunteer time and money to refurbish military-owned aircraft that the government still has authority over the aircraft.

In the case of the Air Force, regulations prohibit government funds from being used to restore aircraft for display purposes. And even though it is legal to allow private groups to spend their own funds on the restoration, the government still retains title to the aircraft, unless legally sold. In Denver, the Air Force still owned the B-29 and exercised its right to do what it pleased with the plane after it was restored.

The Lowry B-29 was caught up in an odd series of events triggered by last year's announcement that the base would close on October 1, 1994. The Air Force Museum office at Wright Patterson AFB in Ohio began making plans to disperse the Lowry aircraft collection, which it owns.

The Lowry Heritage Foundation, which oversees operation of the museum and also restoration work there, moved quickly to formulate a plan to make a civilian museum of the Lowry collection.

The Air Force was not impressed with the foundation's original plans for moving the museum and in the meantime promised the B-29 to the Seattle museum which features Boeing aircraft.

The Air Force said it was concerned for the preservation welfare of the B-29 in light of the uncertain future for the Lowry museum.

Disgruntled Lowry volunteers believe there was some behind-the-scenes politicking involved in the decision. Colorado politicians in Washington, D.C., tried to intercede on behalf of Lowry but reportedly were rebuffed by the Department of Air Force.

While the argument raged, the Air Force moved in, disassembled

The restored B-29 sits beside the Lowry Museum prior to its move to Seattle. - photo by Kevin Corbley

the bomber and trucked it to Washington state.

Ironically, late in the summer, plans for the new Lowry Museum seemed to solidify and the remainder of the 20-aircraft collection probably will stay in Denver at the new museum to be called Wings Over the Rockies.

But the loss of the B-29 has left a bitter feeling with many of the 200 men and women who worked on the 11-month restoration project in 1986-87.

Russ Tarvin, president of the museum's foundation, flew in a B-29 crew in World War II and assisted in rebuilding the plane. His primary gripe with the Air Force is that they let volunteers use their own time and money to salvage the bomber from China Lake and haul it by flatbed trucks back to Colorado. Then the Air Force turned around and decided they couldn't keep the plane they had resurrected, according to Tarvin.

Lance Barber, an Aurora, Colo., resident who was one of the 100 or so regular volunteers is bitter about the bomber's move, but not solely because of his own personal loss.

"My main frustration here is [the Air Force's] disregard for the meaning and mission that plane represents to Lowry and to the volunteers who put it back together," he said. "That B-29 is as close as possible to a living history as you can get to the memory of the men and women who served at Lowry."

Barber refers to the airplane as a representation of Lowry's role as a bomber training base for B-29 pilots and crews in World War II. That particular B-29 is not believed to have served at Lowry.

Many of volunteers who worked on the project did serve at Lowry, and several were from B-29 crews.

"That plane represents a history of Lowry," according to Barber. "At the Boeing museum [in Seattle] it will be just another airplane."

Barber said that when the plane was originally salvaged, the Boeing museum was contacted to assist in the restoration but was not interested.

Lowry's B-29 is identified as "T-Squared 54." Barber explained that the T stands for 498th bomb group of the 875 bomber squadron within the 21st bomber command of the 20th Air Force. The square represents the 73rd bomber wing. This B-29 was the 54th plane in the squadron.

The B-29 flew more than 30 missions over Japanese territory in World War II.

Later it was converted to a tanker and continued war service. After the war it was essentially junked at China Lake and used for target practice by the Air Force.

In November 1986, the Lowry volunteers retrieved it and spent the next year working to restore it.

The plane was in pretty bad shape, and had to be hoisted on new tires. Coors Brewing Co. of Golden, Colo. donated aluminum, presumably recycled beer cans, as a new skin for the plane.

The props were straightened and holes in the fuselage patched. Wings, flaps, vertical stabilizer, flaps and bomb-bay doors had to be entirely reconstructed.

The bomber's distinctive canopied nose had to be completely refabricated with fiberglass and sheet metal. Cockpit instruments were either dummied, or originals were used when they could be found.

Barber and other volunteers have admitted at least some personal disappointment over the plane's loss.

"When you sweat and bleed and bust your knuckles over something and enjoy every minute of it, it becomes a very personal project," Barber said.

Chapter 11

John Bond

John Bond was born on November 3, 1921 in York, Pennsylvania. He was the older of two boys born to Jacob Raymond Bond, a machinist and Anna Margaret Bond. (nee Fisher). Both the Bonds and the Fishers resided and prospered in York for several generations before John was born.
John spent the twenties and thirties in York, graduating from William Penn High School in 1940.
In response to the nations needs, John Bond enlisted in the army on 28 Sept. 1942. Since he was under 21, his parents signed for him. He remained at home until 28Feb. 1943 when he was called up and told to report to Nashville, Tenn. and assigned to Class 43K Aviation Cadet School. He was sent to Maxwell, Alabama for pre-flight cadet basic (6 weeks). Training took him to several bases including Jackson, Tenn., Walnut Ridge, Ark., Waco, TX. and La Mesa, TX. He did not complete his pilot training and on 10Jan,1944, he was sent to Lowry Field and assigned to the 21st Tech. School, SQDN. K, Lowry II, Armament School. It was here at Lowry in Jan. 1944 that he met his wife Grace Cook. Grace (called Cookie) was the daughter of Joseph E. Cook, a noted Denver judge. They were married on 30 Dec., 1945.
On 14 May, 1944 John was assigned to the 3705 AAF Base Unit, (TS) Section R, Lowry I, Remote Control Turret Mech. School and on 21 Aug. the same year he was assigned to Remote Control Turret Repairman School. John was promoted to Cpl.

In Nov. He left Lowry heading for Grand Island, Nebr. Following Grand Island, He was transferred to several training facilities including Tinker Field, Oklahoma City, Stinson Field, San Antonio, Davis Monthan field, Tucson ending up in Camp Stoneman, CA. (A.F. Overseas Depot) The war had ended and he was transferred to Victorville, CA and to Camp Beale Separation Center where he was discharged on 20Feb. 1946. In 1945, John was promoted first to Sgt. on 23Jun and then to Staff Sgt.17Sep.

John stayed in the inactive reserves and as a civilian he and his wife moved to Denver where he realized a boyhood dream. While working at Hayden Field north of Denver, he obtained his private pilot's license.

In May 1946, The Air Force wanted him back so on 17May he was transferred to active duty at Ft. Leavenworth Pers. Processing Center and posted to the AAF Assembly Sta. Det., Topeka AA Field, KS, 4Jun. After a short stay in Topeka, John was assigned to Alamogordo, N.M. 231 AAF BU where the Bond family obtained their first gov't. quarters. On 1Oct., John returned to Lowry for the second time for Clerk Typist School, finishing out 1946 in Denver.

John began 1947 at Andrews AFB, Washington D.C., 64th AAFBU (SAC) Prov. WAC, then on 8May to Keesler Field, Biloxi, Miss. for Airplane Eng. Course, (P-80). and in Sept. to Chanute Field, Class 10017, Aircraft & Engine Mechanic School. On 17Nov., he was again sent to Andrews and stayed until 25Apr.,1949 as crew chief with TDY to Fairbanks, Alaska, Ladd AFB.

25Apr., He transferred to Langley AFB. 4th Fighter Group, with TDY to Anchorage and Ft. Leavenworth. (prisoner transport).

On 25Sep., he was transferred to Vance AFB in Enid, Okla. until May 1950. While in Okla. John and "Cookie's" second child was born, a son Rick (first child Debbie was born in Denver in 1947, the Bonds were to have two more children, Drusilla born in 1952 in Alaska and Becky born in 1954 in Clovis, N.M.). Six Bonds, 6 different birthplaces.

May 26th, 1950 saw the Bonds off to Elmendorf AFB, Anchorage and assignment to the 64th Fighter, Interceptor SQ, 57th Fighter Interceptor Wing, where he stayed until June 1953, as crew chief.

During that time (March, 1951), John was promoted to T/SGT.
On 26Jun.,1953, John was transferred to Clovis, N.M. and was First/SGT for the 4445th Air Base SQDN., with TDY to Amarillo for F-86F training. (1 month)
On Oct., 1954, John was promoted to M/SGT.
On 25May, 1955 John was transferred from Clovis to Lowry AFB, assigned to HQ. USAFA, Chief of Maintenance Section to prepare for the dedication of USAFA, 11Jul. 1955.
1Nov.,1955 - 31Mar.,1961, he was assigned to the 7625th Operations SQDN. USAFA, Flight Chief. During that time, TDY to Chanute, for Wt. Balance Tech. Course and March AFB to attend the NCO Academy. He was assigned on 31Mar.,1961 to the 3417 Consolidated A/C Main. SQDN. (ATC), Lowry.
Transferred 11Jul.,1961 to 66th TAC Recon. Wing, Loan, France until 11Aug.,1963 as crew chief
John finished his service career at Cannon Field, N.M. with the 832 Air Division.
John Bond retired from active duty USAF on 1Sep.,1964, serving 22 years, 24 days during which he was on 42 bases either assigned or TDY, including Alaska and France.
The Bonds settled in Denver and John began work at IBM in the Quality Engineering Dept. in 1965 retiring in 1988.
He joined the Lowry Heritage Museum in 1989.
Besides his love of country and family, John Bond had a third love, singing. It started at the age of 17 with a local church choir and the local theatre players. In high school, he sang in the glee club. On arriving at Lowry, he sang in the glee club, the chapel choir and the local Episcopal church choir.

Wherever John traveled in the service, he sang in the base musical groups and the local civilian organizations. In Alaska, he sang in the Anchorage Community Chorus and sang a solo in the air base production of "South Pacific".

When stationed at Lowry from '55 to 61, John sang solo and in the chorus with the Aurora Civic Chorus and with the Denver Post Operas in Chessman Park. When the Bonds settled in Denver, John sang solo and chorus with the Empire Lyric Players (Gilbert and Sullivan) and several chapel choirs.

John has been the Wings Historian and Photo Archives Director since the museum's inception (12/1994).

Note: John Bond was one of a very few to serve for the entire length of the existence of the 7625th Operation Squadron, USAFA (1955-1961)

Addition to Chapter 11

There is a story that M/Sgt. John Bond tells with pride about July 11th, 1955, the day the Air Force Academy began. It took place at Lowry AFB, the interim location of the academy.

It begins at 6 AM on the 11th as Bond arrives at Lowry in his class A uniform to assist in the inauguration. Passing by the barracks buildings to get to the academy headquarters, he hears ATOs (Air Training Officers) shouting orders at one another, practicing for the day's ceremonies. Arriving at academy headquarters, he encounters a young man who asks "Is this where cadets register"? "I have been here all night to be the first cadet to register." The young man was Valmore Borque, actually the first cadet to register at the US Air Force academy.

Bond's assigned duty for the day was to facilitate cadet movement around the base. While outside of headquarters, he is joined by M/SGT. Kirby. Cadets in civilian attire with baggage begin to gather. The sergeants decided to escort the men to the barracks to meet their ATOs and to be trained for the day's ceremonies. They also decided that Bond would take the first group. Bond called out, "Anyone know how to march?" Several hands raised, ROTC students. Again Bond called out, "Fall in a column of threes.Forward March". Parents who had just recently separated from their sons began waving and applauding. Movie cameras were whirring. Bond felt proud leading this first group.

They marched to the barracks occupied by the training officers. Bond called out, "Halt", "Right Face", "At Ease". Approaching an officer, Bond reported, "Class of '59, Sir". Post, was the officer's reply. Bond was later reminded that officers were to march the cadets. By mistake, John Bond was the first in Air Force history to march Air Force academy cadets.

Sadly, there was another "First" for Borque. He was the first USAFA graduate to be killed in action. His C-123 was shot down by antiaircraft fire delivering supplies to troops near the Cambodian boarder. He was 28.

M.Sgt. John R. Bond (this book's coauthor, at far left) and M.Sgt. Patrick A. Kirby (second from left) greet cadets of the Air Force Academy's first class on July 11, 1955. Valmore A. Bourque (third from right in white suit) was the first cadet sworn in and also became the first combat casualty.

80

↑ BORQUE

Appendix 1

Fairmount Railway

The Fairmount Cemetery was founded in1890. Transportation from the city of Denver was a problem from the beginning. In 1867, the Denver Horse (horse and mule) Railroad Co. was among the first to provide public transportation. The Short system was first to use a form of electricity. This did not prove workable and in 1885, railway companies switched to proven electricity. The next year, 15th street had a scheduled system. Companies often reverted to horse when electric systems failed. Many small companies merged and by 1888, there remained only two, the Denver City Tramway and the Denver City Cable Railway. In 1890, the trolley became the vehicle of choice with overhead cable.

In 1891, in an effort to connect to the existing lines, Fairmount inaugurated horse drawn hack service. The hack began in Fairmount and ran north on Hyde Park (now Quebec St.) to 8th avenue to meet the line from the city. The conductor was Dennis Tirsway. Service began on Sundays but soon increased to daily, Apr. to Nov. Tirsway initially used one horse but due to pressure from the ASPCA increased to two. The cemetery became a place for family outings in addition to visit departed relatives. Finding the horse drawn hacks only somewhat reliable and being rejected by several rail companies, Fairmount began to think about creating a steam line of its' own. On May 30th, 1893, the Fairmount Railway(steam) inaugurated service running from the cemetery up Quebec St. to 7th Ave. west to East End Blvd. (now Poplar St.) then north to Center St. (probably 8th) connecting with the car from the city. Cost - $7775.

Service continued to be a problem, repairs were expensive. In 1896, the line became electric, run by the Colfax Ave, Electric Co. On 23Apr1896 a letter was submitted to the Denver Board of Public works stating that Fairmount and the Colfax co. had come to an agreement and requested that the line switch from steam to electricity at least by Memorial Day of that year since the Grand Army of the Republic was planning a great celebration. On Sundays of that year, the Fairmount Railway Assoc. reported transporting five to eight hundred people on the line. Unfortunately, the Colfax Co. was having financial problems and service again became less than expected.

In 1898, the Denver Consolidated Tramway took over the line. It wasn't until 1900 and considerable more expense for the cemetery, that the line and the connection to the city finally ran smoothly.

   Ref: Fairmount and Historic Co., D. F. Halaas,1976

Engineer William Wesley Goodsell and the Fairmount steam engine, 1895.

Appendix 2

Air Force One

Although President Theodore Roosevelt was the first president to ride in a plane, he was not in office. (post presidency) It was not until 1933 that the government purchased an aircraft for presidential use.

Douglas Dolphin – RD-2 1933-1939. No evidence that Franklin Roosevelt ever used it.

Boeing-314 Clipper #18605 In 1943, The Dixie Clipper transported Pres. Roosevelt to the Casablanca Conference. Franklin Roosevelt was the first president to fly in a plane.
During W.W.II, a modified B-24 was proposed and rejected, partially because of its poor safety record.
Douglas – C-54C "Skymaster" W.W. II named the "Sacred Cow", transported Roosevelt to the Yalta Conference in 1945.

 Pres. Truman also used the "Sacred Cow" until 1947.
Douglas – VC-118 "Liftmaster" 1947 Truman named the plane the "Independence" (Eagle Nose). Truman signed the National Security Act of 1947, creating USAF while on the plane.
Lockheed – C-121A Constellation (round windows, plane number 48-610)

"Columbine II" was in service from 1/53 to 11/54. It was the first to be designated Air Force One. Used to Transport Ike to Lowry. ('53, '54)

Lockheed – C-121E (square windows, plane number 53-7885) "Columbine III" 11/54 to 1959, used for Ike's '55 visit to Lowry. Both the II and the III were Eisenhower's planes. They had western style interiors.

Boeing – VC-137 (a 707) 1958 to 1990, SAM (Special Air Mission) 970, 971, 972.

VC-137C "Stratoliner"- (707-353B) Modified for long range flight began service in 1962 SAM 26000. At this time, Air Force One took on its present color scheme. Another VC-137, SAM 27000, replaced SAM 26000 in 1972.

Boeing – VC-25 (a 747-200B, modified) 1990 to the present.

 SAM 28000 and 29000. President George H W Bush was first to use the VC-25. It was ordered and built during the Reagan administration. Nancy Reagan designed the interior.

Boeing – 747-8 next Air Force One. Contract signed in 2015 for possible delivery in 2017.

The SAM (Special Air Mission) number is the call sign when the president is not on board and is designated on the tail of the aircraft. When the president is on board the call sign is Air Force One.

File:USCG Douglas RD2 June1932.jpg

Clipper leaving for Europe from Marine Terminal, La Guardia Airport

**RD2 DOUGLAS DOLPHIN — ROOSEVELT
NEVER USED**

DIXIE CLIPPER — ROOSEVELT

**DOUGLAS VC-54C SACRED COW
ROOSEVELT, TRUMAN**

**DOUGLAS VC-118 INDEPENDENCE
TRUMAN**

VC-121A COLUMBINE II EISENHOWER

VC-121E COLUMBINE III EISENHOWER

BOEING VC-137 (A 707) EISENHOWER
KENNEDY, JOHNSON, NIXON, FORD,
CARTER, REAGAN

BOEING VC-25 (A 747) BUSH, CLINTON,
BUSH, OBAMA

BOEING 747-8 TO BE DELIVERED IN 2017

Note – The photo of the Douglas Dolphin is same model as the one purchased for President Roosevelt. The other photos are of the actual plane

Appendix 3

7625th Operations Squadron

USAFA

The mission of the 7625th Operation Squadron was to provide adequate flying time for all rated officers of the USAFA and to provide aircraft to the flying Training Dept. of the academy for the purpose of cadet navigational training.

On 8 August, 1954, the first aircraft, a helicopter, was ordered to Lowry for use by the academy.

The original idea was that Lowry was to maintain and service these aircraft and also to provide enough flight time for the academy. It soon became evident, however, because of the rapid increase in rated personnel and the number of administrative flights that it would be impossible for Lowry to fulfill its obligations. It was decided therefore to form the Academy Flight Operations Section, under the Deputy Chief of Staff/Operations.

 In January, 1955, the assigned air craft (4) were transferred from Lowry to the Academy Operations Section.

From January to March 1995, Capt. Russell Tyler was the Officer-in-Charge being replaced in March by Major Harry J. Copsey.

With the establishment of the Operations section, the number of aircraft grew by June to 19, including bombers, trainers and fighters.

In October 1955, the Flight Operations Section was removed from the Deputy Chief of Staff/Operations and on 13 October 1955, the 7625th Operations Squadron was created by GO 43, and assigned to the Air Force Academy, Major Copsey commanding. The authorized strength of the squadron was 10 officers, 135 airmen and one civilian. Aircraft strength was 31 aircraft. By May 1956, aircraft assigned totaled 40 and included a C-131, one H-19, B-25s, F-86s, T33s, 2 C-47 and a T-29s.

The squadron performed all necessary functions except field-maintenance support which was done by Lowry Air Force Base. Due to the age and condition of some of the aircraft and the lack of depot maintenance, repairs and the AOCP (Aircraft out of commission due to lack of parts) plagued the squadron for much of it's existence. Innovation, substitution, professionalism and hard work proved to be the answer.

In Sept.1958, when the academy moved to it's permanent location, cadets and staff returned to Lowry to continue training and flying.

With the reduction in flying at Lowry and the transfer of flying activities to Buckley and Peterson, the job of the 7625th also decreased.

On 7 Oct.,1961, Air Force personnel were transferred to Lowry AFB by Special Order 212. The 7625th Operations Squadron was deactivated following the transfer order.

Insignia of the 7625th Operations Squadron

Acknowledgements

The authors wish to thank Wings Over the Rockies Air and Space Museum and several anonymous donors for their financial support without which this document would never have seen the light of day. We felt the nature of this book precluded any contract with a commercial publisher. We turned to the museum and they responded with the right answer. We owe them and others a debt which we doubt we will ever be able to repay. We also wish to thank members of the second floor gang at the Museum: George Blood who started the ball rolling by commenting one day, "This should be mandatory reading for anyone that works at the welcome desk," and who guided one of us (G.P.) through cyberspace, Lance Barber a long time volunteer at the Wings Museum and the Colorado Aviation Historical Society(colahs.org), a good friend with limitless knowledge and enthusiasm, Ron Newburg, who even volunteered to print a spiral version of the book with his own equipment and Jack Ballard, our associate in the photo archives section, whose advice was and is always indispensable.

Bibliography

Ballard, J. S., J. Bond, G. Paxton *Lowry Air Force Base.* Charleston: Arcadia, 2013.

Epler, Frederick J. *Lowry AFB Flight Operations, A Chronology.* Lowry Heritage Museum, 11/17/1989

Halaas, David F. *Fairmount and Historic Colorado*. Denver: The Fairmount Association, 1976.

Hamrick, Michael F. "History of Bombardier Training at Lowry Field, Colorado, 1940-1941", Aurora: Columbia College Aurora, Colorado, Research Project, 1987.

Harper, Frank. "Colorado's Forgotten Airbase, The Original Lowry Field, 1924-1938". Colorado Heritage Magazine, Autumn 1994, 2–11.

Haulman, Daniel L. *USAF Humanitarian Airlift Operations. 1947-1994, Washington, D. C.: Air Force History and Museum Program, 1998.*

Levy, Michael H. *Men for a Mechanized Army, Lowry Air Force Base in World War II, parts I and II*. Denver: Office of History, Lowry Training Center, n.d.

Levy, Michael H. and Patrick M. Scanlan. *Pursuit of Excellence,*

A History of Lowry Air Force Base 1937-1987. Denver: Lowry Technical Training Center History Office, 1995.

Lindbergh, Charles A. *We.* New York: G. P. Putman's Sons, 1927.

Nankivell, John H. *History of Military Organizations of the State on Colorado, 1860-1935. Part 9, 417 - 425,* Denver: Kistler Stationary Co., 1935. The data on the 120th Observation Squadron is available at Photo Archives, Wings Over the Rockies Museum.

Noel, Thomas J. *Richthofen's Montclair.* Boulder: Pruett Publishing Co., 1978.

Scamehorn, Howard L. *First 50 Years of Flight in Colorado.* Denver: University of Colorado Bulletin #2, History Series, 1961.

Denver Post, Rocky Mountain News. Both papers were used and quoted as a result in doing research for the book. For the most part, when a specific item is noted, the date of the article is stated in the text. Both papers are available at the central branch of the Denver Public Library

Rev-Meter, Lowry Airman. A similar process was used for these references. An extensive collection is available in the research library of Wings Over the Rockies Museum.

Index

George Paxton is a retired pediatrician. He was born in New York City, attended Columbia University and Boston University, School of Medicine. He moved westward in fits and starts, stopping at Whitesburg, Kentucky for one year to do general practice for the United Mine Workers and two years in North Dakota on the Standing Rock Indian Reservation for the United States Public Health Service. He acquired his pediatric training at The Children's Hospital in Denver, Colorado. After six and a half years of private practice in southwest Denver, he joined the West Side Neighborhood Health Program (part of President Johnson's war on poverty). He retired in 1991. He is married, has six children, ten grandchildren and three great grandchildren. He joined the volunteer crew at the Wings Museum in 2004.